THE WAY IT WAS

SANTA BARBARA COMES OF AGE

Front Cover: *Postcard of 400 block of State Street circa 1900. (Courtesy of Santa Barbara Historical Museum; thanks to Bill Dewey)*

Back Cover: *(top to bottom) The 900 block of State Street circa 1926 with the Bothin building in left foreground and the Granada Building in the distance; Howard-Canfield Building on 800 block of State Street circa 1905; the 100 block of East Carrillo Street circa 1926 with the El Castillo Building (left) and Masonic Temple. (Courtesy of John Fritsche)*

Front End Papers: *A 1902 view of Santa Barbara from the Mesa shows Carrillo Street on the left and Canon Perdido Street on the right. (Courtesy Library of Congress)*

Back End Papers: *A view of State Street circa 1904 shows Our Lady of Sorrows with its new bell towers in the background and the intersection with Canon Perdido Street in the foreground. (Courtesy Santa Barbara Historical Museum)*

Title Page: *State Street circa 1890, when Santa Barbara was still a Wild West town with wooden sidewalks and dirt streets with hitching posts, and public transportation consisted of stages and mule-drawn trams. (Courtesy Santa Barbara Historical Museum)*

PHOTO CREDITS: The vast majority of photos in this book come from the **Santa Barbara Historical Museum's Gledhill Library** whose extensive photographic collection documents the rich and varied history of Santa Barbara. All other sources of images are listed with the captions.

THE WAY IT WAS
Santa Barbara Comes of Age
Copyright 2017 by Hattie Beresford

Printed by Sinclair Printing Company, Los Angeles, California

First Edition: 2017

ISBN: 978-0-692-94842-2

THE WAY IT WAS

SANTA BARBARA COMES OF AGE

Hattie Beresford

Many Thanks

To **Michael Redmon**, director of research at the Gledhill Library of the Santa Barbara Historical Museum, who is always encouraging and ready to help and rarely complains about lugging up those heavy bound archives of the *Morning Press*.

To the Buckley family of the *Montecito Journal*, especially to **Tim Buckley** for helping and shepherding me along the path to this book, and to **Trent Watanabe** for his excellent design and infinite patience. To **Guillaume Doane**, for hiring me in the first place and setting me on this wonderful course.

To the late **Maria Herold** of the Montecito Association History Committee, who took me under her wing back in 2002 and taught me Montecito. (I wish the plane had never landed, Maria.)

To a woman I never met, the late **Stella Haverland Rouse**, whose many history columns for the Santa Barbara *News-Press* have been carefully archived at the Santa Barbara Historical Museum. Her interests were as eclectic as mine, and she always gave dates -- an important clue for finding primary sources of information. Her work is excellent and accurate, and one of her columns, coincidentally, was called The Way It Was.

To **John Fritsche** and **Dr. C. Seybert Kinsell** for sharing their memories and their postcard collections. These collections of images are invaluable sources of historical information for Santa Barbara County. My articles been much enriched by their generosity. To **Judy Pearce**, who schlepped me along to meet long time residents and hear their stories and told a few of her own. May you always wear a daisy in your hair. To **Kathi Brewster** for her generosity in sharing her vast knowledge of local history and setting me on the right paths.

To **Trish Davis** and the "gang" at the Montecito Association History Committee Room (at Montecito Hall) for always being so friendly and welcoming and for allowing me to utilize images and information from their excellent archive.

To the late **Jim Blakley**, for the many times he shared his notes, his photos, his oral histories, and his memories as I trod the historical trails leading into the mountains.

Dedicated

with love and gratitude
to my husband Michael,
my first reader and staunchest supporter.

Introduction

I've always been drawn to historic places; they exude a special ambiance, fostered, perhaps, by the evidence of the work and lives of those who came before. My heritage probably has something to do with it. I was born in the nearly two-hundred year old *Het Lissabon*, a courtyard community in The Hague, Netherlands. Nothing to get too excited about when you realize that the Dutch word for courtyard is *hofje* which also means poorhouse. Actually, *Het Lissabon* was a relatively new neighborhood compared to the *hofjes* in Leiden where my father grew up. They had been occupied by the *Mayflower* Pilgrims before they abandoned Dutch-speaking Holland for the New World.

One of my favorite childhood memories is of holding my grandmother's hand as we walked the cobbled and brick Denneweg past the glamorous Hotel des Indies to the Binnehof, the 500-year old Dutch Parliament building that sits in the *hofvijver* or moat. Parliament held no interest for me, but the white swans floating majestically in the *hofvijver* gathered at the stonewalls for the crusts of stale bread my delighted four-year-old self tossed to them.

Then, when I was nearly five-years old, we immigrated to the United States, ending up in suburban Southern California. Everything was new, and our home lay among the thousands of acres taken up by postwar stucco dwellings in North Hollywood. There were no swans, but we did have a big backyard and our own private swing set and a blow up swimming pool. Sundays at Zuma beach, summer hide and seek with neighborhood kids, swim parties, … it was a great life, but there was something lacking, and I was too young to know what.

I ended up going to UCSB, and after getting a teaching credential I accepted a position in Santa Barbara. Here was a town with a historic core; a town that valued and protected the remnants of its varied, and sometimes checkered, past. Able to finally dig deeper into that past after my retirement, I began to read and research the stories behind the development of this beautiful and special place. Here was a town that had preserved its old Spanish mission and many of its original adobes. A town that recreated, meticulously and authentically, its Royal Presidio, demonstrating a reverence for an earlier time and culture. A town that revered and protected its historic buildings and homes.

The history of Santa Barbara's Chumash, Spanish, and Mexican days has been researched, preserved, and presented by dozens of excellent historians and organizations such as the Santa Barbara Mission, the Museum of Natural History, the Trust for Historic Preservation and the Santa Barbara Historical Museum. We know how Santa Barbara grew from village to pueblo to town, but how did we develop into the town we have today. What forces shaped our destiny. Those were the questions whose answers I sought.

Though a few wealthy Easterners were driving automobiles in the 1890s, the first car didn't arrive in Santa Barbara until 1901, so I wondered, how did the advent of the automobile affect this horse and buggy town. I have been hiking the front and backcountry trails for years, and I wanted to know the stories of earlier trail travelers and residents of our canyons. Santa Barbara loves its celebrities, and I became curious about the town's celebrations of famous early visitors. Perhaps most importantly, I wanted to know the stories behind the people whose time, energy, vision, and/or beneficence determined the shape and culture of our town. All this wondering led to research, and that research brought forth some fascinating facts and stories about Santa Barbara's past. Over the past 12 years the *Montecito Journal* has kindly allowed me to indulge my eclectic curiosity in the writing of some 300 articles on local history, and the Santa Barbara Historical Museum has allowed me to use historic photos to augment these stories. These photos are invaluable documents of the way it was in Santa Barbara. The 18 stories included in this volume take the reader back to Santa Barbara's growing years, the years of 1880-1930, when the ambitious little town developed the underpinnings for the town we know today.

I hope you enjoy this trip to the past.

Hattie Beresford

Table of Contents

Section One

Rolling out the Red Carpet

❦

From the 1883 visit of Queen Victoria's daughter, Princess Louise, through all the visits of U.S. presidents and domestic and foreign dignitaries thereafter, Santa Barbara has rolled out the red carpet with enthusiasm and verve.

In 1891, the stopover of President Benjamin Harrison inspired a floral parade and battle of the flowers to honor his brief visit. The event was so successful that from 1892-1896, Santa Barbara hosted a weeklong flower festival to celebrate the horticultural riches of the area. In 1901, President William McKinley stopped by for a three-hour date with Santa Barbara, followed in 1904 by President Theodore Roosevelt.

The Great White Fleet made Santa Barbara a port of call in 1908, and the citizenry went into a frenzy of preparation for the multi-day celebration.

During a 1919 diplomatic visit to the United States, Belgium's King Albert and Queen Elisabeth paused in Montecito and Santa Barbara for several days to enjoy a respite from staged events. Despite orders to keep their sojourn casual, Santa Barbara couldn't help itself and put out a hospitable welcome mat regardless.

In April of 1939, Crown Prince Frederik and Princess Ingrid of Denmark visited both Santa Barbara and Solvang. Modern times saw President Reagan establishing Santa Barbara as the "Western White House," and Queen Elizabeth of Great Britain waving hello in 1983. A helicopter delivered Prince William and Catherine, the Duke and Duchess of Cambridge, to Santa Barbara in 2011. Kate watched from the grandstands as William played in a game of polo at the Santa Barbara Polo Club.

Over the decades, Santa Barbara has also welcomed its share of top-name entertainers. From Gilbert and Sullivan operettas to the chorus lines of the enormously popular and sensational *Florodora*, Lobero's Opera House was often filled to the brim. The circus was also a yearly visitor, but none drew more enthusiasm than the 1902 visit of Buffalo Bill's Wild West show.

Following are the stories behind five such historic visits.

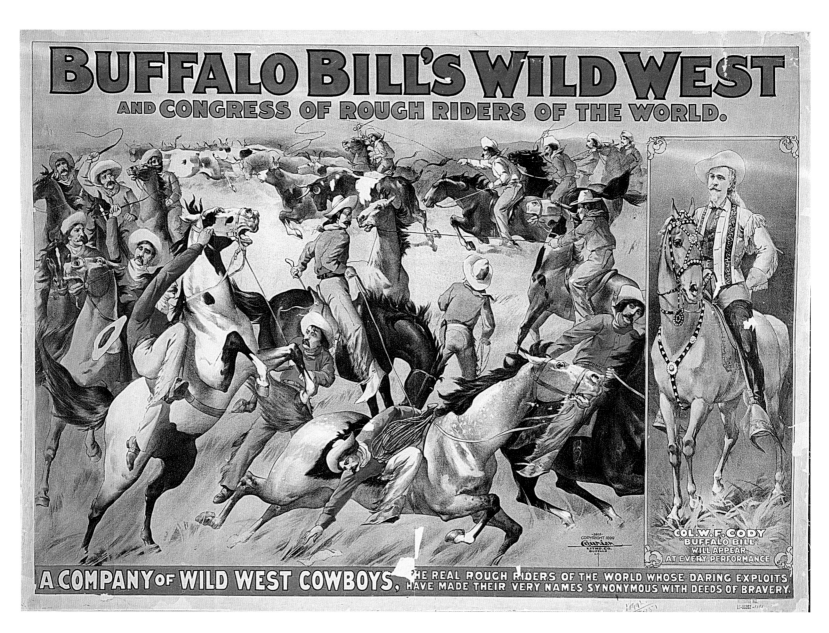

Colorful, action-packed posters like this one announced the upcoming arrival of Buffalo Bill's Wild West show in each and every town on the schedule.
(Library of Congress)

Buffalo Bill and His Wild West Show

William F. Cody sits for a studio portrait. (Library of Congress)

"**N**o circus ever called together such a crowd as that which found its way to the Agricultural Park yesterday afternoon and evening on the occasion of Buffalo Bill's first visit to Santa Barbara," reported the *Morning Press* on September 23, 1902. More than 7,000 people rushed to find seats in the covered stands surrounding the arena that the Wild West show had set up in the middle of the race track of the Agricultural Park, which once lay between Cabrillo, Salsipuedes, Montecito, and Santa Barbara streets. Santa Barbara's population being less than 7,000, the crowd was augmented by hundreds of wagons and carts conveying residents from the country areas and a special train carrying nearly 400 Venturans.

Major John M. Burke, the Wild West's publicist, had come to town earlier in September to make arrangements, order provisions from local businesses, and publicize the show by placing ads in the local paper, plastering the town with posters, and granting interviews to the local press. Burke assured reporters that everything in the show was real and genuine. The Cossacks were real, for instance, not Americans rigged out for the part.

Colonel William F. Cody dubbed his show *Buffalo Bill's Wild West and Congress of Rough Riders of the World* at its inception in 1883. In 1898, the press corps borrowed the term "Rough Riders" and bestowed it upon Roosevelt's Cavalrymen during the Spanish American War. Afterward, the Wild West hired 16 veterans of Roosevelt's regiment for the show. For the 1902 performance in Santa Barbara, a reenactment of "The Battle of San Juan Hill" was the featured closing spectacle, replacing "Custer's Last Stand."

A special train from Bakersfield arrived in Santa Barbara the night before the performance, and an army of cowboys, Sioux Indians, sharpshooters, lariat throwers, and Bedouin Arabs set up camp. Several hundred head of livestock, including one of the largest groups of bison still left in the

The race track of the Agricultural Park lay on the Middle Estero and was frequently flooded, but the expert crew of the Wild West show managed to create a spectacular venue out of the normally soggy park.

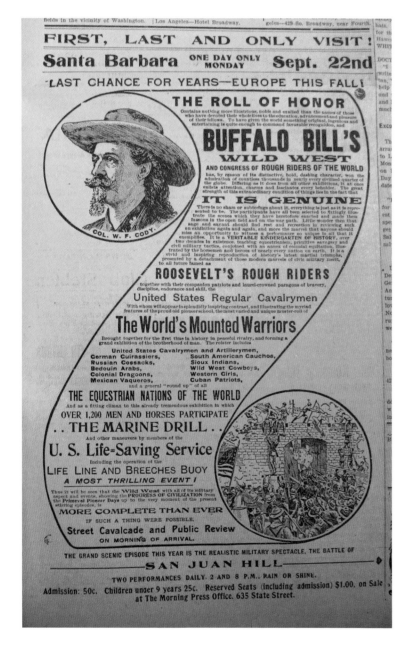

Major John M. Burke, Cody's publicist, came to Santa Barbara to place advertisements like this one.

nation, debarked the train and were corralled.

The show's electric power plant was set up, and two 20-foot-long portable ranges fed the 400-member cast and crew three hot meals a day. The entertainment arena was the largest in the world, capable of seating 16,000 people. So efficient was the Wild West's system that Kaiser Wilhelm of Germany had assigned special agents to the show in order to learn how to move his armies more efficiently.

Creation of a Legend

Born in Scott County, Iowa, in 1846, William Frederick Cody embarked on his adventurous life at age 11 after the death of his father. Young Cody set out to augment the family income by working as a bullwhacker for the railroad and then as a mounted messenger for a freighting firm. At 13 he took part in the Colorado gold rush, panning unsuccessfully for placer gold, and later trapped beaver for a season. In 1861, at the tender age of 14, he became a pony express rider. At 15, he joined a jayhawker group, a Civil War guerrilla group loyal to the Union. Ashamed of his participation in this unsavory operation, he enlisted in the regular army.

After the war, he married Louisa Frederici and tried to settle down as a stage driver and then as a hotel manager. He quickly gave up this docile life, however, and hired on as a buffalo hunter for the railroad, shooting 12 head a day from horseback at a sporting run and earning the nickname "Buffalo Bill." In 1868, he became chief of scouts for the Fifth Regiment U.S. Cavalry and was a participant in the U.S. victory at Summit Springs during the Indian Wars.

His reputation caught the imagination of the East, and Ned Buntline became the first to write one of nearly 700 dime novels about Buffalo Bill's exploits. When the army saw Cody's potential as a public relations boon, they commissioned him to guide European dignitaries on excursions and hunting trips throughout the West. None was grander than the full-scale media event surrounding the visit of the Grand Duke Alexis of Russia. Cody's career took a new turn; he started touring the country in stage plays that portrayed his past exploits.

Among the many foreign dignitaries whom Cody guided through the Rocky Mountains was the Prince of Monaco. (Library of Congress)

The Wild West Show

In 1883, anticipating Frederick Jackson Turner's frontier thesis by a decade, Cody developed Buffalo Bill's Wild West show in Omaha, Nebraska. In 1893, Turner claimed, "… the frontier has gone, and with its going has closed the first period of American history." Cody wanted to make sure the frontier era was remembered, so he created an extravaganza that was an appealing mix of documentation and showmanship. Claiming absolute authenticity, the show presented the public with wagon trains, pony express riders, Sioux Indians, elk, bronco busters, and sharpshooters. Famous battles were recreated, settler's cabins attacked, and the Deadwood stage was ambushed.

After seeing the show, Mark Twain wrote to Cody and said, "It brought back to me the breezy, wild life of the Rocky Mountains and stirred me like a war song. The show is genuine–cowboys, vaqueros, Indians, stagecoaches, costumes, the same as I saw them in the frontier years ago."

The show traveled to London in 1887 for the American Exhibition, and the Europeans went wild. In 1889, the Wild West returned to that civilized continent for a four-year tour that was immensely popular. Rosa Bonheur, the notable painter of animals, frequented the Wild West camp in Paris, making sketches and taking notes. She painted the famous image of Cody atop his white horse, Tucker, which, in one form or another, graced many subsequent advertising posters.

The show was no less popular in the Eastern states where the dangers and rough life of the frontier had faded into legend. With the Indian "menace" gone, it was safe to admire the bold unfettered life, which was especially appealing in light of Victorian strictures. That nearly 20 years would pass before the Wild West would make its debut in the Far West is no surprise. The Far West had to be tamed and civilized before it could look back with nostalgia. The *Morning Press*'s droll assessment, however, was, "…the West learned much about itself as it is presented by Buffalo Bill and Company."

Cody's publicists gave him credit for teaching the artistic community that horses were not stiff creatures standing on two legs and never galloped with their legs spread wide in the air. Apparently both Frederic Remington and Charles Schreyvogel, among dozens of others, owed Cody a great debt. Today, some historians credit Cody with perpetuating the folklore of the West and inventing superstardom. Others say he laid the foundation for the entire western genre of books and movies in the twentieth century.

The Wild West in Santa Barbara

*I*n 1902, Santa Barbarans and their visitors were not interested in scholarly analysis and debate. Instead, as September 22 dawned, a feeling of childlike anticipation pervaded the town as the street cavalcade of stagecoaches and wagons and world renowned mounted warriors wended

D. F. BARRY,
WEST SUPERIOR,
WIS.

SITTING BULL AND BUFFALO BILL.
Copyrighted 1897.

Cody's company included many famous Native Americans who traveled to Europe with the show. (Library of Congress)

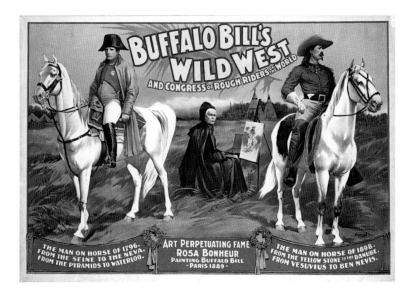

The Wild West show spent many years in Europe where artist Rosa Bonheur created the classic image of Cody astride his white horse, Tucker. (Library of Congress)

their way up State Street. The public marched alongside, and exuberant young boys broke into leaps and sprints of excitement.

Each of the two shows in the magnificent arena opened with Buffalo Bill's Cowboy Band playing "The Star Spangled Banner," long before it became the national anthem in 1931. (Another possible credit to the Wild West show.) Clad in wide-brimmed hats, chaps, boots, and long-sleeved shirts and studded gun holsters, the band played march tunes and ragtime and popular songs. The music accompanied the show, filling in during the change of acts and influencing audience response to the performances by expressing the moods of each scene.

From the safety of their seats, Santa Barbarans witnessed incredible feats of horsemanship and the colorful costumes of the South American gauchos and Russian Cossacks. The sharpshooters and lariat throwers amazed, the Marine Drill instructed, and the Indian dancers evoked a primal pulse. The recreation of the Battle of San Juan Hill inspired patriotism, but best of all, Buffalo Bill's riding and shooting brought the

audience to their feet.

The ad poster had warned, "First, Last and Only Visit," and, indeed, it was, since the show returned to Europe for four years in 1903. In 1913, after 30 years of delighting audiences, the company went into receivership. Though Cody joined the Sells-Floto Circus and returned to Santa Barbara in 1914 and 1915, the days of the Wild West show were over. Bufflao Bill died in January 1917 and was buried atop Lookout Mountain in Colorado.

Paul Libman and Dave Hudson's lament for the musical, *Dust and Dreams*, expresses the loss, not just of Cody himself, but by extension, the American frontier as well.

"Buffalo Bill is gone;
Everyone knows the score.
Buffalo Bill and his Wild West Show
Won't be thrilling our hearts no more."

Thus ended an era that shaped the nation and the national consciousness.

Buffalo Bill paraded the Rough Riders down State Street before the first performance in Santa Barbara.

The men from the 16 battleships of the Great White Fleet paraded on West Cabrillo Boulevard and passed the reviewing stands at Plaza del Mar. In keeping with the theme, the muzzles of their rifles sported stems of flowers, a different flower for each ship.

The Great White Fleet

As the band played "The Girl I Left Behind Me," an unprecedented stately procession of 16 white battleships with gilded scrollwork passed before the presidential yacht *Mayflower* in the waters off Hampton Roads, Virginia. Hampton Roads, today's Norfolk Naval Base, had drawn more than 1.2 million visitors that year for the 1907 Jamestown Exposition celebrating the 300th anniversary of the founding of the first successful English colony.

Intended to show the world the wonders the United States had accomplished in industry, education, art and science during the previous 300 years, the Exposition was the perfect site from which to launch the new Atlantic Fleet. Roosevelt believed that only a strong navy could project the nation's power and prestige abroad. Having recently acquired the Philippines, Guam, Puerto Rico, and a naval base at Guantanamo Bay, and busy constructing the Panama Canal,

President Theodore Roosevelt on the Mayflower off Hampton Roads during his review of the Atlantic Fleet at the start of their round-the-world voyage. (Library of Congress)

Roosevelt felt that a show of naval power in the Pacific was needed to protect American interests.

Though promoted as a diplomatic mission, the round-the-world cruise was seen by many as an example of Roosevelt speaking softly and carrying a big stick. Many in California welcomed the big stick, however, hoping it would send a clear message to Japan to limit emigration. Others feared it would provoke Japan to attack and imperil the fleet at the treacherous Strait of Magellan.

Later nicknamed the Great White Fleet, 16 battleships made the 14-month journey with 14,000 sailors, four auxiliary supply, tender, and repair ships, and a torpedo flotilla of six early destroyers. Starting out on December 16, 1907, they traveled 43,000 miles and made 20 ports of call

A view of the fleet from oil magnate William Miller Graham's estate called Bellosguardo. It was replaced by a new mansion in the 1930s by the Anna LaChapelle Clark, widow of copper baron and former U.S. Senator William A. Clark.

on six continents.

At their first port of call, December 23 through 29, they were snubbed. The governor of Trinidad, who had been ordered to ignore them, commanded that all Christmas parties and celebrations be cancelled so as not to seem welcoming. Thereafter, however, they were greeted warmly in Brazil, Chile, and Peru. As the fleet continued its northern course in the Pacific, it was slated to make several ports of call in California, including one in Santa Barbara.

Dressing for the Ball

As the date for the fleet's arrival drew near, Santa Barbara was all atwitter in its determination to give the very best reception in all of California. The committee of artists who directed plans for the Floral Parade and Battle of the Flowers included Stewart Edward White, author; Rob Wagner, portraitist; Fernand Lungren, painter of desert scenes and moody nocturnes; and Charles Frederick Eaton, an artist and landscape architect who had initiated the great Flower Festivals of 1892-'96. Also on the committee were ardent civic promoters Joel Remington Fithian, co-owner of the country club, rancher, and son of a prominent businessman; John F. Diehl, world-famous grocer; and Augustus B. Higginson, noted architect.

The Flower Festival Committee called on private citizens to take in paying guests and notified restaurants and other vendors that 30,000 meals a day were needed. The *Santa Barbara Independent* trumped the *Morning Press* by installing a wireless receiver and contracting with the Navy to receive and relay communications from the ships of the fleet, and the Home Telephone Company planned to lay a cable from the shore to the flagship *Connecticut*.

Artist Alexander Harmer created this advertising poster for the festival that would welcome the fleet.

Police Chief James Ross warned citizens to lock all doors and windows, conceal valuables, and keep porch lights on all night to deter the criminal element that was likely to invade the town. A squad of detectives from Los Angeles arrived to help the local police spot pickpockets and other unsavory characters. Mayor Elmer Boeseke exhorted citizens to clean up their yards, their houses and their streets.

A mosquito fleet comprised of 10 launches from Long Beach arrived to ferry citizens out to the fleet and sailors into Santa Barbara. The local Japanese community raised money for daytime fireworks to welcome the fleet, and bands from Santa Maria, San Luis Obispo, and the battleships themselves were scheduled to play concerts at Plaza del Mar.

A call went out for floral ammunition for the Battle of the Flowers. From Goleta to Carpinteria, flowers could be placed at collection stations along the road where they would be gathered by automobiles and delivered to the Boulevard tea house which served as the armory for the event. As the day grew nearer and floral contributions were slow to arrive, the *Independent* exhorted the citizenry to "Bring in Your Flowers! This Means Everyone! Strip Your Garden for the Occasion–The Blossoms Can Never Be Put to a Better Use!"

Plaza del Mar, the Boulevard (West Cabrillo Boulevard), and State Street were awash in decorations. A great canopy

Dozens of boats ferried thousands of people out to the Great White Fleet anchored in the Santa Barbara Channel. (Courtesy Dr. Seybert Kinsell)

Alexander Harmer painted the festive scene of the Battle of the Flowers.

of foliage and flowers was erected at the corner of State Street and the Boulevard. Merchants vied with their neighbors to create attractive window displays although Trenwith's violet-decorated cart drawn by a white Teddy bear clearly won everyone's heart. Red lanterns festooned the streets, the Plaza, and the Potter Hotel grounds. Thousands of gay pennants lined the parade route while red, white, and blue bunting, banners, and flags blanketed the town. The city was ready!

The Fleet Arrives

On April 25 the shoreline, hillsides, and cliffs were crowded with people hoping to catch the first glimpse of the Great White Fleet. Shortly after 2 p.m., a thin strip of black smoke emerged from the soft mists to the east. The wisps increased in number until the first of the ships emerged from the foggy shroud followed by another and another until all 16 steamed along the shore in perfect

As a bevy of Santa Barbara women trotted by in floral bedecked carts, flower girls cheered them on while the admirals of the fleet and festival organizers watched from an awning-covered dais. Spectators perched in the bandstand, on rooftops and in every place imaginable at Los Baños del Mar.

formation until they reached their anchorages. Then, they turned as one to face the city.

The *Morning Press* reported, "At precisely 4:30, sixteen anchors sank with a splash, the great anchor chains rattling with a booming clattering noise that reached the shore as one concerted volume of sound; sixteen engine crews reversed screws and brought sixteen monsters, beautiful, majestic in peace but terrific in strife, to a full stop." The fleet had arrived.

Launches set off immediately to transport the reception committee of Mayor Boeseke, retired Rear Admiral Bowman H. McCalla, and the executive committee of the Civic League to the *Connecticut,* where they officially welcomed Rear Admiral Charles M. Thomas and the Atlantic Fleet.

The accompanying surge of barks and boats racing to

see the giant battleships did not go without mishap. John S. Edwards, Ruth and Samuel Spaulding, and a Miss Wood narrowly escaped death when their catboat, *Volga,* was cut in two by the *Nellie,* a tugboat out of San Pedro. The young people managed to throw themselves into the drink before the collision and were rescued, none the worse for wear, by the crew of the tug.

That night, and every night thereafter, thousands of tiny lights illuminated the ships, and dozens of searchlights frolicked over sky, land, and sea.

Launches ferried thousands of people to the fleet where they investigated every nook and cranny of the magnificent ships. As more and more people arrived by special trains and by automobiles, the Civic League was hard pressed to find

All 16 ships streamed along the shore in perfect formation until they reached their anchorages and turned as one. (Courtesy Dr. Seybert Kinsell)

The admirals of the fleet and town dignitaries watching from the reviewing stand at Plaza del Mar included (left to right) retired Rear Admiral Bowman H. McCalla in the white hat; Rear Admiral Charles M. Thomas, commander-in-chief of the Atlantic Fleet; Santa Barbara Mayor Elmer J. Boeseke; an unidentified admiral; and Floral Parade director Rob Wagner. (Courtesy John Fritsche)

accommodations for all who wanted them. Private citizens rented out rooms, and hundreds of cots were put in the lobbies of the hotels.

Everyone awaited Monday, the day of the Floral Parade honoring the officers and men of the Atlantic Fleet, the Battle of the Flowers, and the first night of dancing under the stars on the Boulevard.

Feting the Great White Fleet

On Monday April 26, flower-bedecked carriages conveyed the admirals of the fleet to the reviewing stands on the Boulevard. Forest rangers provided an escort, and young girls from the oldest Spanish families offered floral ammunition for the ensuing Battle of the Flowers.

Leading the parade on horseback was grand marshal, John Edward Beale, accompanied by his aides wearing Spanish costumes. Then came the sailors, 64 from each ship; dressed in pure white, each group sporting a different flower

The women of Santa Barbara gave as good as they got in the Battle of the Flowers.

Joel Remington Fithian provided a carriage that Alexander Harmer designed and decorated to convey the admirals of the fleet to the reviewing stands. On its second trip, the carriage was filled with descendents of the De la Guerra family, one of the city's founding families.
(Courtesy Dr. C. Seybert Kinsell)

in the muzzles of their rifles. Next came marching children, bands, and clubs after which flower-gilded carts, carriages, automobiles and floats took over the scene.

C.W. Dewlaney's Ford runabout was transformed into a meadow of wildflowers outlined by California poppies. Several thousand calla lilies transformed W.J. Willat's touring car into a replica battleship, complete with a gun turret that could shoot flowers. The High School contributed Minerva, the goddess of wisdom, and the Chamber of Commerce contributed Saint Barbara, who was accompanied by grey-clad Franciscan monks intoning Gregorian chants.

And so it went, one elaborately decorated carriage after another paraded past the tribunes. When they returned for another sweep of the route, the battle commenced.

Armed with nosegays of colorful blossoms, the officers in the reviewing stands bombarded the elegantly dressed women in the carriages with a shower of bouquets. The *Independent* reported, "Many a delicate hat was set rakishly over its

owner's eyes by a well-directed blow, but the Women of Santa Barbara, never to be defeated, arose at every hand and gave better than they had received."

When the last carriage drove off, the officers indulged themselves in a battle among themselves. They jumped into the street and kept a hail of missiles falling. The *Independent* revealed that even Admiral Thomas entered the fray, firing "a broadside of blossoms that exploded over the heads of the officers, and they returned fire until the admiral was literally raked with blossoms of as many hues and varieties as Santa Barbara can grow."

That night, the Boulevard was swept clean, and the sailors were treated to an open-air band concert and dance. Of the dozens of private parties intended to fete the officers of the fleet, the tea hosted by Admiral and Mrs. McCalla at *La Casa Santa Cruz* and the grand ball at the Santa Barbara Country Club's new clubhouse (on the site of today's Music Academy of the West) were the most spectacular.

Swabbie Entertainment

While the officers attended one elegant affair after another, the average swabbie danced under the stars on the Boulevard. So popular was this activity that many nights they were joined by the officers who'd been released from more formal gatherings.

During the day, the sailors explored the city. Some hired horses and indulged in races up and down State Street. One group was taken for an auto tour and was offered large bags of oranges to disperse to fellow shipmates. These showed up at the Potter Theater at a performance of "The Rambling Rose" where the sailors enlivened the entertainment by joining in the songs and showering the prima donna with flowers, oranges and lemons, which they rolled upon the stage by the dozens. It was all in good fun.

One incident, however, marred the otherwise perfect visit. Storekeepers, liquor dealers, and restaurant proprietors had been warned not to raise their prices at the risk of losing their licenses. One restaurant owner, John Senich of 121 State

Swabbies enjoyed late-night street dancing, theater performances, and sporting contests against local athletes.

Local businesses had been warned not to raise their prices or they would lose their licenses. This owner lost much more when he charged a group of sailors five times the normal rate.

Street, lost much more. When two sailors were charged more than 6 dollars for two small steaks, a dozen oysters, and two bottles of beer, all of which normally totaled $1.30, the sailors reluctantly paid. Later, however, they complained bitterly to their shipmates.

Outraged on behalf of their compatriots, a group of sailors, armed with pikes stripped of the pennants decorating the Boulevard, descended upon the then-closed restaurant. They hesitated at the sight of the red, white, and blue bunting, banners, and flags. Then, someone carefully removed the patriotic trappings, and the sailors set in with a vengeance. Before the provost guard with their heavy hickory sticks could get there, the rioters had obliterated the place. Senich claimed it had all been a misunderstanding, but he came under severe criticism from the town.

On a lighter note, the *Independent* reported that a small group of sailors had been listening to the wheezy tunes of a hurdy-gurdy playing dance music on an uptown street when they became inspired and began to dance, each by himself, wide trousers flapping at their heels and dreaming of pretty girls to dance with. From the dark, a sweet female voice rang out in the night air, "You sailors ought to be ashamed to dance alone."

Startled, the sheepish sailors turned to face their critic only to behold a group of belles from the previous night's Santa Barbara Country Club ball standing before them.

"We'll dance with you; we'll dance with anyone that wears that uniform—won't we girls?" said the girl who had spoken before.

Soon the couples were gaily waltzing to the tune of the hurdy-gurdy man. As the song wound down and faded into the night air, the sailors bowed to their partners, and the girls giggled merrily as they strolled off arm in arm to their homes near the Mission.

The Dance of the Flowers

Neither the *Independent* nor the *Morning Press* could find sufficient verbiage to praise the "Dance of the Flowers" presented to more than 2,000 officers of the fleet at Plaza del Mar on Wednesday evening. Artist Elizabeth Eaton Burton, had been tapped to design the costumes and the dance.

That evening, the twinkling lights were doused, and a

Mrs. Stewart Edward (Betty) White wears a lily costume designed by Elizabeth Eaton Burton for the Dance of the Flowers.

beam of violet light created a pathway upon which 24 lithe young women, dressed as flowers, entered the stage. The lights came up again as they performed a ballet to the slow, graceful rhythms of Ethelbert Nevins' "Narcissus." Later, Senorita Ynez Dibblee y de la Guerra represented Spring in a whirlwind of movement. The show closed with the 13 figures of the Contradanza, a tribute to Santa Barbara's Spanish heritage performed by children descended from the founding Spanish families.

On Thursday, the great ships sailed away before most of the city awoke. Only a few early souls witnessed the fleet weigh anchor at 6 a.m. and steam silently and sedately northward in a single column four miles long. After a few more ports in California, it turned west into the open Pacific to complete its round-the-world cruise. Santa Barbara was deservedly well-satisfied with her role in the historic event; she had rolled out the red carpet and acquitted herself superbly.

Lillian Beale (later Child) at the reins, and artist Elizabeth Eaton Burton, who created the Dance of the Flowers, trot along the Boulevard during the parade for the Fleet.

King Albert, Queen Elisabeth and Crown Prince Leopold arrive in Hoboken, New Jersey, on October 2, 1919. (Library of Congress)

King Albert of Belgium's Sojourn

A poster welcomes the representatives of warworn Belgium to the United States. (Library of Congress)

When Germany agreed to an armistice on November 11, 1918, thereby ending The Great War (WWI), Belgium found itself among the most devastated of European countries. Military action accounted for more than 65,000 deaths of soldiers and civilians and another 55,000 died of famine and disease. Belgium's industries lay in rubble, its farmland in waste, and whole neighborhoods ceased to exist.

On October 2, 1919, the U.S.S. *George Washington* docked at Hoboken, New Jersey, and landed King Albert and Queen Elisabeth of Belgium along with their son, Crown Prince Leopold, and a royal retinue of 37. The first guests of the U.S. government since Lafayette laid the cornerstone on the Bunker Hill Monument a hundred years earlier, they planned to spend 26 days on a coast-to-coast visit of the nation.

When President Wilson proved to be too ill to see the Belgian delegation, King Albert cancelled most of his Eastern tour and decided to head for California. Herbert Hoover, former chairman of the Commission for Relief for Belgium, arranged a last-minute visit to Santa Barbara for the royal suite.

Secretary of State Robert Lansing advised Santa Barbara Mayor Harvey T. Nielson that the King wanted the visit to be low-key. The telegram stated, "The King is going to Santa Barbara to be perfectly quiet and desires

After WWI, much of Belgium lay in ruins like these at Ypres. (Library of Congress)

to have no official reception or recognition…. You are advised that the king will be incognito while in Santa Barbara. You are requested to observe the above suggestion to the fullest extent."

Well, Santa Barbara tried but it was just not in her nature to be inhospitable. As the special 12-car train raced across the continent with a crate full of "buttons" (then-slang for kingly medals), "low-key" plans in Santa Barbara proliferated.

Speeding Across the Continent

On the westward journey, rather than reposing in sedate seclusion as befitted his station, Albert proved that he was just a "regular guy" and no ordinary king. He had studied journalism and worked for several newspapers before assuming the crown, and he was known to travel incognito to various spots in Belgium to assess problems and situations for himself.

When the special train crossed into Ohio, King Albert climbed into the locomotive and took the throttle for ten miles. As they sped through the grain fields of the Midwest, the King said he was not unmindful of the food they had sent to his starving people in the desperate days of the war. And he paid homage to the gallantry of Ohio's 37th Infantry Division and the significant part they played in delivering Belgium from the Central Powers.

At Cheyenne, Wyoming, Albert climbed into the engine cab to sit behind the engineer for the long ride through the moonlight. When they stopped in Sparks, Nevada, Albert was missing when the engineer called "All Aboard." He had gone for a walk up the tracks and lost sight of time. At Truckee, Albert and his son climbed aboard the first of the two engines that dragged the train up the grade. They ate lunch with the railroad men and then climbed on top of a baggage car for a better view of the canyons, mountain peaks and mining towns of the Sierras.

Herbert Hoover secured the use of Casa Dorinda, the estate of Anna Dorinda and William Henry Bliss, for the royal family.

King Albert was well respected for his "hands on" involvement in ruling Belgium for the benefit of the people. (Library of Congress)

After reaching Sacramento, the train turned south and reached Santa Barbara at precisely 9:06 a.m. on Saturday, October 11, when the royal party was greeted by thousands of cheering Santa Barbarans. Whisked away in several cars, the King and his retinue were delivered to Montecito, where two estates had been secured for their use. King Albert and family stayed at *Casa Dorinda*, the newly-completed mansion of William Henry and Anna Dorinda Bliss in Montecito. Much of his retinue stayed at *Mira Vista*, the estate built by I.G. Waterman in the 1890s.

Highlights of the Visit

To honor the King, city officials renamed the almost-completed "Round the City Boulevard" (today's APS) as King Alfred Boulevard. The *Morning Press* was impressed with Queen Elisabeth's gray walking suit and "snappy gray turban with two tassels hanging over the side around which had been flung a fluffy white veil. The veil, an open effect, shielded her entire face and had been brought down tight under the chin and then folded and tied behind."

After settling in at *Casa Dorinda*, King Albert gave the lie to his desire to be "perfectly quiet and left entirely alone" by heading for the Miramar where he plunked down 25 cents for a bathing suit and plunged into surf while Queen Elisabeth watched from the beach. The royal party's four days in Santa Barbara were filled with touristic activities.

Prince Leopold went for a motorcycle ride and spent half his time trying to make the machine run. The rebellious bike ran in spurts and emitted black smoke and noise, once throwing the prince to the ground. According to the *Morning Press*, he returned to the Bliss estate "dirty, greasy, and thoroughly happy."

Meanwhile, C.K.G. Billings offered King Albert the use of Uhlan, his world-champion trotter. When the King went for his first ride on the record-setting steed, he found Sheriff James Ross guarding the gate. In his memoir, Herbert Hoover writes, "At that time, Santa Barbara still maintained a Hollywood sheriff with a ten-gallon hat, high boots, and two revolvers." Ross's attempt at addressing the king properly was a comic "O

King Albert rides C.K.G. Billings' famous trotter, Uhlan, along the beaches of Santa Barbara.

King" instead of "Your Majesty," but Albert found it endearing and assured the sheriff that it was perfectly correct. The two rode together daily and, according to Hoover, the two became devoted to each other. The sheriff was inducted into the Order of Leopold I when their time together ended.

The King and Queen flew to the Channel Islands in the F-1 seaplane built by Malcolm and Allan H. Loughead. They were suitably impressed with the Santa Barbara landscape, which reminded them of parts of Italy and particularly of Nice.

Albert was fond of walking and hiking and included those activities in each of his days. One day found him walking from *Casa Dorinda* to *Solana*, the Frederick Forest Peabody Estate, where he dropped in quite informally and had tea with Frederick.

Another day, Albert and his hiking companions had reached Las Canoas Road when the king became thirsty. His aide approached the little frame cottage belonging to Hattie Brinkerhoff.

Caught in a time-warp of the 1890s, complete with

King Albert carries the dusters and Queen Elisabeth sports a flyer's helmet in preparation for their flight in the Loughhead F1 seaplane over the Santa Barbara Channel. (Richard A. Heath/Early Lockheed history collection, SBHC, Mss 76, UCSB Library, Department of Special Research Collections)

Gibson girl hairdo, high-button shoes and a corseted wasp waist, Hattie was used to being teased. (Once the police chief jokingly gave her buckboard a parking ticket.) So, when a stranger knocked on the door and asked for a drink of water for the King of Belgium, she chuckled and pointed to the pump. This jokester could help himself, and, a bit taken aback, he did. Eventually, the truth dawned on Hattie and she was completely mortified. Nevertheless, she ended up naming her little canyon King Albert Glen in honor of the visit.

A Whirlwind Tour of Town

From visitations to the three premier hotels in town (Potter, Arlington, and El Mirasol) to planting redwood trees at Alameda Park to picking walnuts in Goleta, Albert and his queen saw it all. Visiting the Recreation Center, he especially wanted to see the building where so many things had been made for his country during the war. The Red Cross building, built for $9,000 by members of the Red Cross in 1917, would find its peacetime use as a gymnasium.

Though women were usually forbidden in the sacred garden of the Santa Barbara Mission, Queen Elisabeth was invited on a tour during which she ceremoniously planted an orange tree.

The American Red Cross
wants clothes to send over-seas
to Belgium and Northern France

*Phone The American Red Cross-
Greeley 5650 (24 west 39th St.)
and they will tell you how—*

The Recreation Center and later the Red Cross building on Carrillo Street saw hundreds of volunteers working to help the wartorn countries of Europe. (Library of Congress)

A tour of the Flying A studios treated Albert to a screening of a film taken during his flight in the Loughhead (Lockheed) seaplane the previous day. The select audience chuckled at the antics of Agent Bill Nye as he attempted to protect the king from the adoring mob.

On Sunday, a special mass was held for the King at the mission after which the royal family was invited into the sacred garden, special dispensation being given the Queen since women were not normally allowed in the cloistered area. She

earned the honor by ceremoniously planting an orange tree.

The last day of the King's visit was a busy one. Up at 6 a.m., the royal family hiked to *Mira Vista,* and, gathering their retinue, tramped across country to the Bothin place in the hills. Breakfast was prepared out of doors and eaten by a blazing campfire. Then the King rode horseback over Cold Springs and Hot Springs trails before taking the royal family to *Arcady* where the party swam in George Owen Knapp's indoor Roman pool.

After an afternoon swim at the Miramar, Albert rode Uhlan on the beach while the tide was out. The *Morning Press* reported, "They made a wonderful picture, the tall, soldierly king and the beautiful black Uhlan…."

By 10 p.m. that evening, the visit was over, and the train chugged out of the rail station headed for San Francisco and King Albert's official welcome to California. At the end of the month, hopefully reinvigorated by his time in Santa Barbara, he was back in New York and Washington, D.C., working to secure assistance for Belgium's recovery in the form of loans and business relations.

Albert and Queen Elisabeth, seen here shaking hands with First Lady Edith Wilson, finally had their audience with the President upon their return from California. (Library of Congress)

(Left to right) Secretary of State John Hay; Postmaster General Charles Emory Smith; Santa Barbara Mayor Charles A. Storke; Secretary of the Navy John D. Long; former Santa Barbara mayor and chairman of the welcoming committee Frank Whitney; and President William McKinley at the public reception at the Arlington Hotel on State Street

McKinley Madness

Spectators join the parade to the Arlington Hotel for the public reception that would underwhelm a young Edward Selden Spaulding.

May 9, 1901. With President William McKinley scheduled to arrive the next day for a three-hour visit, Montecito and Santa Barbara were all aflutter. The *Morning Press* took on the role of town crier, peppering the pages with last minute, almost hysterical, reminders, such as:

"Citizens, revamp those derelict flagpoles; fly the flags high. Merchants, organize flower drives and bring them to the command post in your wagons. Teachers, assemble the children between Figueroa and Victoria. Everyone, bring flowers. Everyone, small flags can be had for a penny; bring them. Red Alert! The presidential carriage decorating committee has only half the pink Duchesse roses needed. Go cut some and bring them to the decorating tent!"

Civic primping reached manic proportions. Santa Barbara was like a country belle preparing for her first suitor. Even the train crew got into the act. The engineers and firemen frantically rubbed, painted, burnished, and petted Engine 1457 until, as the *Morning Press* reported, "when evening came, she bore a greater resemblance to a rainbow-hued comet than a thundering horse of steel." The pilot bars and smoke stack were painted red, white, and blue. A picture of McKinley, wreathed in boughs and blooms of his native state, hung over the boiler number plate and Old Glory was draped on either side of the tank. The engine crews chose white uniforms with brass buttons so they'd be as spick and span as their engine. Even the coal was handpicked so it would be the purist coal available.

The President Arrives

May 10, 11 a.m. The special train carrying President McKinley stopped at the State Street crossing and the President disembarked without the first lady who was seriously ill and remained aboard. Former mayor Frank Whitney escorted the President to his carriage, which had been specially decorated by artist Elizabeth Eaton Burton.

Pink Duchesse roses against a background of gray moss were complemented by driver Alfred Ortega and footman Stephen Valenzuela, costumed in pink and white. A team of four white horses plus four outriders similarly attired completed the striking effect. A shower of roses filled the

The presidential cortège at the railroad crossing on State Street as it heads toward the Arlington Hotel. (There would be no State Street station until 1902.) The President was escorted by the Sixth Division, Naval Militia of Santa Barbara, and was showered with blossoms by cheering spectators along the route.

air when the President took his seat. Several other blossom-bedecked carriages conveyed his entourage up State Street to the Arlington Hotel through a gauntlet of waving flags and a barrage of floral missiles.

After the obligatory "Rally Round the Flag" speech in which McKinley stated, "A splendid civilization comes cut from the old states and from the old nationalities represented here today–the best civilization in the world," the public lined up to shake his hand. The reception, however, was cut short since time was of the essence.

Many people were disappointed when McKinley was whisked into the dining room to partake of a special luncheon feast with the most prominent citizens of Santa Barbara and Montecito. One woman, having missed shaking his hand at the Arlington Hotel, later ran up to him at the Santa Barbara Mission and touched his coat. "There," she was reported as saying, "I've touched him anyhow!"

At lunch, Mrs. Mary B. Spaulding, wife of banker and civic benefactor Edward R. Spaulding, sat in for Mrs. McKinley. The rest of the party sat in order of rank. Course after course came out, and, in less than an hour, President McKinley was expected to consume an endless array of dishes. Blue point crabs, celery, salted almonds, and consommé were followed by boiled salmon with Hollandaise sauce,

President McKinley addresses the crowd at the Arlington Hotel.

President McKinley and cabinet visit the cemetery at the mission.

cucumbers, stuffed olives, and chicken patties *à la Reine*. Then came McKinley punch, asparagus, boiled squab, lettuce salad, American flag ice cream, fancy cakes, Roquefort cheese and black coffee.

Reluctant to return to his floral conveyance, McKinley requested a more sedate equipage for his trip to the mission. Elizabeth Eaton Burton and friends were more than happy to take charge of the floral masterpiece they had created and set out to tour the town in high style.

At the mission, McKinley was given a tour of the sacred garden whose grounds were forbidden to women. Mrs. McKinley was to have been only the third woman for whom an exception would have been made. The President visited the church and the ancient graveyard and then hurried off to the Victoria Street Station where crowds had gathered to present him with presents and bouquets. Dr. Francesco Francheschi, world-famous horticulturalist, offered a bouquet of delicate tropical flowers, and artist Etta Sanders presented a burnt leather-work pillow created in her studio on State Street.

Engine 1457, having replaced the previous engine, was steaming majestically as it stood ready to convey the President on the next leg of his journey. As the train lurched forward, the President stood on the tailgate and waved his handkerchief in adieu. Santa Barbara's three-hour date with President McKinley was over.

As Seen by a Boy

Like the country maid reporting on her outing with the local swain, the newspapers put the very best spin on the occasion. Weren't we wonderful! Wasn't he! Young boys see differently and perhaps more clearly.

Edward Selden Spaulding, son of Edward R. Spaulding and, later, founder of Laguna Blanca School, was 10 years old when McKinley arrived. His family was invited to join the cavalcade of carriages escorting McKinley and his party to the Arlington Hotel. Their carriage, brightly decorated with yellow acacia blossoms, carried Postmaster General

At the patriotically bedecked Arlington Hotel, Mayor Charles Storke welcomes President McKinley.

McKinley is treated to a tour of the sacred garden at the mission.

Charles Emery Smith and his wife, and was driven by the family coachman, Archibald Ballentine. Seldon later reported in his memoir that "Bal" was one of the most distinguished whips of the community. Their two big, glossy blacks with luxurious tails and manes had been gentled by Ballentine through years of careful handling.

Seldon said a keen rivalry developed between the carriage owners as to which one would be able to bring his team so close to the railroad car that the dignitary who was to ride with him would be able to step from the railcar directly into the carriage.

"When the presidential train approached, and then slowed down to a stop, men yelled and cheered enthusiastically, whistles blew, and steam spurted in great clouds from the engine," wrote Spaulding. "It was all very stimulating! Certainly it was all very stimulating to the horses drawn up to receive the incoming guests! They did everything but fly in their frantic efforts to leave the area."

Despite the attentions of four men at the heads of the

white horses of McKinley's carriage and a competent driver in the box, nothing could make these horses approach the rail car. "In the end," wrote Spaulding, "to the mortification of everyone, the President was required to descend to the ground, to walk across the intervening space, and then to climb into the waiting coach."

The second driver had no better luck, and then it was the Spaulding coach's turn. "Bal took our fine, gentle blacks up to the side of the train at a smart trot and stopped them so close to the iron steps that the waiting Secretary was able to step directly into the acacia-bedecked carriage! There was a proud

Elizabeth Eaton Burton (second from left) and William Waples Burton (fourth from left) stop the presidential carriage they had decorated in front of the mission at the end of their cruise around town after McKinley had bowed out.

boy in Santa Barbara that day."

Shortly thereafter, at the Arlington, Selden was prodded into a long line moving slowly into the reception room. "This was a new and little understood experience for me," he wrote. "I had but the vaguest notion what it was all about. Presently I found myself standing before a tubby little man of unimpressive appearance. I mean no disrespect whatever to the President, of course. The comparison was with my friend and mentor, Ballentine, a man of strong frame and fine handlebar mustaches."

Still somewhat befuddled regarding the import of the experience, 10-year old Spaulding wandered along with the crowd until one of his elders grabbed him and said, "Selden, when you are an old man, you can tell your grandchildren that you have shaken hands with the President of the United States."

"It seemed," wrote Selden in his memoirs, "that she was taking a lot for granted. For my money, Bal was the greatest horseman who ever saw the light of day.... It is wonderful to be a small boy!"

President McKinley waves a Chatacqua goodbye to Santa Barbara.

Theodore Roosevelt speaks to mounted forest reserve rangers and sheriffs from the steps of the Santa Barbara Mission.

Teddy Roosevelt Rides to Town

(above) President Theodore Roosevelt in the engine compartment of the train approaching Redlands, California. (right) The eagerly awaited presidential train crossing the Rockies (Library of Congress)

When President Theodore Roosevelt visited Santa Barbara on May 9, 1903, he was enthusiastically greeted, but the grandiose effort that had welcomed President William McKinley two years earlier was decidedly lacking. Perhaps McKinley's assassination four months after visiting Santa Barbara made the city err on the side of caution. Instead of floral carriages and a battle of the flowers, and in place of a seven-course luncheon at the Arlington hotel after a public reception, Roosevelt had a guard of 24 forest rangers and eight mounted sheriff deputies in addition to 20 police officers on patrol.

Roosevelt's two-month tour of the West, from April 1 to

Theodore Roosevelt lays out his plans for the nation and compliments the history and beauty of Santa Barbara at Plaza del Mar.

June 5, 1903, was intended to gain support for his legislative program and secure the presidential nomination in 1904. Since custom frowned on a sitting president vigorously campaigning, he would be forced to sit back while his opponents battled fiercely for the nomination. The trip, therefore, was essential to gaining the support of the people.

Santa Barbara eagerly awaited the President's arrival. As the day drew nearer, the *Morning Press* diligently reported his train's westward movement with headlines that screamed, "Roosevelt is in Kansas … in Colorado … in New Mexico … in Arizona … in Redlands."

When the President reached Los Angeles on May 8, two regimental battalions were called out to break up the crush of people pressing the reviewing stand. They used bayonets and the butts of their rifles to literally beat back the crowd. The newspapers reported, "Men fought the soldiers at every step and received cracked heads for their pains. Women fainted." The President cut his speech short and went for a drive.

Though Santa Barbara's plans for impressing President Roosevelt were decidedly more sedate than those for McKinley, organizers did want to present the city well. J.H.R. Wagner, who was in charge, called for donations of date and fan palm branches, which would be placed on the telephone poles along the route for the presidential party. He hoped to make a tasteful palm avenue of the town. Residents along the route were asked to decorate their houses with flags, but bunting and calico were forbidden, being altogether "too excessive." Businesses were asked to close from 11 a.m. to 2 p.m. out of respect for the President.

Arrival at Montecito Station

On May 9, despite the earnest wishes of the citizenry, the dense fog that had plagued the town for a week refused to lift. Twelve carriages drove through a heavy mist to the Montecito Station at Spring Street and Depot Road to greet the President.

Mayor George S. Edwards and Chamber of Commerce president Mr. Thomas D. Wood, rode with Roosevelt in the first carriage. Twelve rangers from the Santa Ynez Forest Reserve led the way, mounted sheriff's deputies surrounded the presidential carriage, and 12 rangers from the Pine Mountain Forest Reserve secured the rear of the cortège. Leaving the Country Club, which was located on the site of today's Biltmore Hotel, the procession followed Olive Mill Road to Sycamore Canyon Road.

Groups gathered along the route to greet the President who smiled and bowed to every person who saluted him. At nearly every home along the beautiful drive through Montecito valley, flowers were strewn in the road. Stopping for a few minutes at I.G. Waterman's estate, *Mira Vista*, the members of the procession stretched their legs on the terraces and endeavored to enjoy the fog-shrouded view.

Then it was over Eucalyptus Hill Road to Quinientos Street where a delegation from the County Poor Farm cheered Roosevelt on. The women of the Eastside, not happy with the organizer's meager plans, had a surprise for the distinguished guests. They had transformed the bridge across Sycamore Creek, the *Morning Press* reported, "into a bower of bloom," and "showered floral tributes in front of the carriages."

When the parade of carriages reached the railroad crossing at Milpas, the train came around the curve when only half the procession had crossed the track. The last driver had to pull up sharply and swing the horses alongside the track to avoid being run over.

At Plaza del Mar, a battalion of 115 sailors from the training ship, U.S.S. *Alert*, plus the local naval militia and members of G.A.R (Grand Army of the Republic), formed an honor guard around the grandstand. The *Alert* boomed a 21-gun salute while the crowd cheered. Roosevelt praised Santa

Barbara, its history, and its beauty. He explained his plans for the nation and called on the patriotism of the citizens to work for the common good.

When Roosevelt learned that famous Western author Stewart Edward White was in town, he invited White to board the train at the end of its stopover so the two could have a longer conversation. White later debarked at San Luis Obispo having forged a firm friendship, and in 1905, Roosevelt would make him a U.S. Forest Reserve inspector.

Heading for the Mission

From Plaza del Mar, a zigzag route led the presidential procession through residential neighborhoods to the mission. At one point along the way, Ruth Cordero, a 7-year-old African American girl from Carpinteria, was

Theodore Roosevelt visits the mission cemetery, hat in hand.

Theodore Roosevelt poses with his Rough Riders in 1898 after the capture of San Juan Hill, where Santa Barbara resident Stanley Hollister was wounded.
(Library of Congress)

carried to the presidential carriage by Colonel Russell Heath, Carpinteria farmer and attorney. She presented Roosevelt with a bouquet of flowers. (Roosevelt had incurred a storm of Southern ire when he invited an African American, the head of Tuskegee Institute, Booker T. Washington, to dine with his family in the White House in October 1901.)

As the President traveled up State Street, an event occurred that validated his heavy escort. As Edward Selden Spaulding recalled years later, "A man in a buggy drove at a fast trot out of a side street and tried to approach the presidential carriage as closely as might be. Seeing this, one of the outriders, Bob Clark of Ventura, spurred forward, seized the man's horse by the left rein close to the bit, and, still at a 'run,' guided the animal into the next intersection. The infuriated driver lashed at Bob's horse with his whip, but he was helpless so long as this fine horseman remained at his horse's head." What the man's purpose had been in this

escapade, Spaulding was never was told.

After a tour of the Santa Barbara Mission, during which Roosevelt lingered longingly in the mission library among its old books and manuscripts, the Rangers presented Roosevelt, who was a staunch supporter of conservation and preservation, with a souvenir. Roosevelt told them, "I think you men are doing one of the greatest works for your country…. In reference to the forest and wild creatures that live in them, I think our aim should be not to selfishly destroy them but to preserve them for our children and our children's children. I thank you for your escort, and I like the way you ride."

Then Roosevelt learned that one of his guards was Harry Hollister, whose brother Stanley had been a Rough Rider at the Battle of San Juan Hill. Stanley had survived the charge only to be wounded in the chest by shrapnel, which had ricocheted off Roosevelt's wrist. As Stanley had made his way to the first aid station, an enemy bullet had fractured his

Annie Hollister was visiting her daughter Jennie Hollister Hale at her home near the Mission when Theodore Roosevelt stopped to speak to her about Stanley.

hip. Even this he survived, and he was evacuated from Cuba to Virginia, where he caught typhoid fever in the hospital and died.

Roosevelt asked to meet with Hannah (Annie) Hollister, Stanley and Harry's mother, who was staying with her daughter, Jennie Hollister Hale, on the corner of Laguna and Pedregosa streets, which lay on the way to Victoria Station, where his train awaited. When he reached the Hale home, Roosevelt stopped the cortège and spoke quietly and briefly with Annie on the lawn of the Clinton Hale home.

Though the meeting was quick, it put the presidential party behind schedule, so the horses were whipped into a trot, and, with the front riders sweeping onlookers out of the way, the procession proceeded at breakneck speed to the train station, where they arrived precisely on time: 2 p.m. A cheering crowd waved Roosevelt on his way north where more speeches and more receptions awaited him. The trip to the West was a success; Roosevelt won the 1904 Republican primary and the election.

Roosevelt's bower covered engine drew the train from Santa Barbara toward Santa Cruz.

Outfitters provided mules for excursions along Mountain Drive, circa 1905. (Courtesy of John Fritsche)

Section Two

Into the Hills

❦

Santa Barbarans have been lifting their eyes to the hills since time immemorial. The canyon trails to the ridge of the Santa Ynez Mountains have been trod by Chumash, Spanish, Californio, and Yankee travelers for hundreds of years.

After the American period began in 1848, homesteaders claimed quarter sections, and outlaws found secluded hideouts in the backcountry. As Santa Barbara matured and law and order became established, picnics in the canyons became popular Sunday activities. In the summer months, whole families would pack up and head for the mountains for several weeks of camping.

In the late 1880s, the Reverend A.W. Jackson visited Santa Barbara and was overcome by its beauty. In *Barbariana*, the book about his travels, he writes," … the mountains shoot up four thousand feet. The sea is in every landscape. The country is undulating. In the fresh season it is clothed in the greenest grass or is aflame with blossoms. Stately live oaks abound; the wide-branching sycamore is here and there. Taken together, … we have here a valley as fair as that in which Rasselas pined…."

Shopkeepers capitalized on the popularity of mountain excursions by advertising alpenstocks, fully packed picnic baskets, and the latest in camping gear and clothing. Horses and mules and guides were for hire. It seemed that the more civilized the town became the more often people sought the solace of nature. Not a summer day went by that the local newspapers didn't announce the comings and goings of groups traveling into the Santa Ynez Mountains.

Trail maintenance was an ongoing problem, however. In 1886, the newly formed Go-Ahead Club, a service group composed of the young people in town, raised money through an evening of poetry, song and recital for the Trail Fund. In the first years of the 1900s, the Chamber of Commerce and the newly-formed National Forest Service became involved in trail and road building and maintenance.

After the introduction of the first automobile to Santa Barbara in 1901, however, many Santa Barbarans exchanged their hay-eating horsepower for gas-guzzling horsepower. Auto camping and excursions into the mountains became popular. Partially in reaction to this automation, a group called The Hikers formed in 1913 and organized day hikes into the mountains, thereby saving the tread on their tires but putting a strain on their shoe leather.

Today, Santa Barbara's front country continues to be popular as an increasing number of residents head to the hills to find what John Muir described as "Nature's peace and refreshment" and to enjoy the spectacular views and natural landscape.

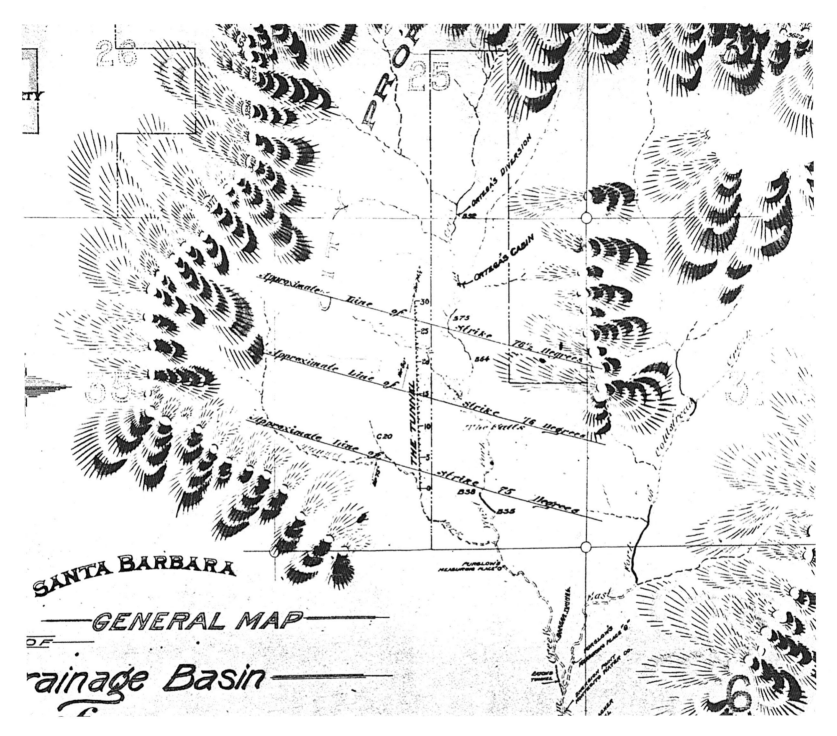

Circa 1902, Cold Spring Creek was called Coldstream Creek, and this map shows the location of several of the tunnels as well as the Ortega homestead.

Cold Spring Canyon Trails

The Barker Tunnel still supplies water to clients today. (author photo, 2007)

Jose del Carmen Romero with his dog Montie riding pillion on his horse Frank along Cold Springs Trail in 1915 (Baker family album; MAHiC)

O ne of the most historic of the front country canyons, Cold Spring Canyon is traversed by three trails. The oldest is the trail that ascends the north fork and reaches the ridge. This trail was established in 1878 when assayer James A. Shedd and two men, two donkeys, and two mules came over from the Los Prietos mercury mines by cutting a new trail that saved several hours of travel time. Shedd and his companions cut brush down from the ridge until they reached the established cattle trail in the canyon.

Traveling the trail in 1885, local writer Edwards Roberts described Cold Spring Creek as flowing in a ravine that grew increasingly narrow as it penetrated deeper into the range. "The banks are low and moss-grown," he wrote, "and are covered with stones and boulders that have been washed from the mountains and are now piled together in wild confusion. At the end of the cañon, near where the valley below and the ocean are visible, the creek leaps over a precipitous wall of rock with a fall of 300 feet [Tangarine Falls]."

In 1904, a local guide to trails said that in the deep ravines of the old Cold Spring Trail grow giant Woodwardia ferns, and from "The Pinnacle," where the waters plunge into the ravine, spectacular views are attained.

In 1898, José Dolores Ortega, a descendent of Don José Francisco Ortega, former commander of the Santa Barbara Presidio, received a patent for a homestead of 160 acres along the upper portion of this trail. Ortega built a 10-foot by 20-foot home of shakes, boards, and poles as well as a corral. He planted 18 fruit trees and rows of grape vines, watering them from a 300-yard long irrigation ditch.

Another canyon dweller was William Joseph Chard, a Santa Barbara butcher. He and his family only lived there a short time as Chard lost out in a dispute over water rights with neighbor James Barker. Chard's wife Dina wasn't dismayed, she hadn't liked living in a snake-infested wilderness. Evidence of their occupation include periwinkle, cactus, and olive trees.

East Fork, West Fork

The East Fork Trail was built by the newly formed Santa Ynez Forest Reserve's rangers during 1902 and 1903. It crosses the ridge and drops down into Forbush Flats and continues on to the Santa Ynez River. It was intended to be the main trail to the pineries in the San Rafael and Sierra Madre ranges. On the south slope, it crossed 367 acres of private land, which the Gould family

Seven years after the 1897 hiking group visited Cold Spring's horizontal wells, hikers were visiting the new tunnel drilled all the way through the mountain from Mission Canyon to the Santa Ynez River.

Alex Dominguez and "Old Steve," caretaker of the Ogilvy Ranch over the mountain, pause at the eucalyptus trees planted by Ferdinand Delbrook near the summit of Cold Spring Trail. (Courtesy Jim Blakley)

donated to the city as a park in 1926.

Ferdinand Delbrook, who lived and worked as a gardener on the Ogilvy estate on Ashley Road, used the trail to pack in cypress and eucalyptus trees to plant on Arthur Ogilvy's backcountry ranch. Ferdinand also planted eucalyptus trees 2.7 miles up East Fork Trail to provide a shady resting place. The Ogilvys' Chinese cook used the trees as a landmark on which to train his field glasses. When he saw the horses and mules clustered near the trees, he knew it was time to start preparing a meal.

The West Fork Trail lies on the northern 150 acres of a private estate and rises up to intersect with today's Gibraltar Road. In the year 2000, the environmental investment group called Cima del Mundo donated a conservation easement to the Land Trust for Santa Barbara County, thereby ensuring that the acreage would not be developed and that the right to use the trail would be guaranteed to the public in perpetuity.

It is along the West Fork Trail that three water tunnels, or adits, were constructed to bring water to a thirsty Montecito and Santa Barbara. The first of these was the Eaton Tunnel, bored in 1892 on the southwest side of the creek at its confluence with the east fork. Charles Fredrick Eaton used the water for his landscape and horticultural business at his estate called *Riso Rivo* (Laughing Rivulet), which is today *El Mirador*. The Barker Tunnel was the second horizontal well dug into the walls of Cold Spring Creek. James L. Barker began boring his adit in 1894 and completed it in 1898.

Since Montecito wasn't alone in needing water to supply a growing population, in 1896 the City of Santa Barbara decided to bore 5,100 feet into the mountain farther up the west fork of Cold Spring Creek. By the time the project was completed in 1903, however, the demand for water had once again outstripped the supply, and litigation over rights to water from Cold Spring Creek flooded the court system. The answer, the city decided, was to bore a tunnel in Mission Canyon all the way through the mountain to tap the waters of the Santa Ynez River, which they would also dam.

No photos have been found of the miners in Cold Spring Canyon, but these miners of Mission Tunnel faced the same discomforts and dangers as their predecessors.

Water collects behind the bulkhead inside Cold Spring Tunnel.

An 1897 Hike

Today's hikers of Cold Spring Canyon are luckier than the group who trudged the West Fork Trail more than 100 years ago. Reporting on an April 1897 outing in the *Morning Press*, one hiker advised, "Ladies will find a stout stick or 'alpenstock,' or even a closed umbrella, of great assistance

Charles Frederick Eaton, noted landscape architect and Arts and Crafts artist, retained the right to water from Cold Spring Canyon to provide water for his estate. Its charming lotus pond was actually a reservoir used to water his citrus grove.

in climbing." (Considering that the ladies were wearing cumbersome long skirts, stout sticks were probably essential.)

When the party reached the Barker Tunnel, which was still under construction, the nearby cabin, tent, and tunnel itself were deserted. Two of the boys had been told that the tunnel contained carbonic acid gas (carbon dioxide), which could easily be detected by a lighted candle extinguishing itself. They decided to conduct a chemical experiment and lit candles as they entered the tunnel. Even after they reached the very end, however, their candles did not go out. When they reemerged, they were somewhat let down by the seemingly uneventful adventure until they discovered that the coins and keys in their pockets had turned black as had a watch completely wrapped in a leather chamois case.

"Imagine their consternation," wrote the reporter, "when they learned of the workman who was overcome and had to be dragged out, and that it was considered so dangerous that those most familiar with it would not enter longer than a few minutes."

In fact, James Barker did not resume work on the tunnel until June of 1897 when a series of mirrors reflecting the sun were installed to provide light and the ventilation system was improved. Despite those efforts, in November, Thomas Curran and Fred Ware, two workers, suffocated on the fumes. When the tunnel reached a depth of 1,250 feet in 1898, it was declared complete. Today, Barker Tunnel water still supplies Westmont College and other properties.

The City's Cold Spring Tunnel

Farther up the trail, the 1897 hikers found Cold Spring Tunnel. Today, the little cabin they found in a charming nook, has long since returned to the elements, and the hubbub of the miner's camp has given way to a quiet rocky glade strewn with russet-colored sycamore leaves

Dissatisfied with the private water company that supplied the town, the Santa Barbara City Council decided to get into the water business for itself. Eugene F. Sheffield donated his land in Cold Spring Canyon, as did Charles Frederick Eaton, who retained the right to 1½ miner's inches of water for his nearby estate.

When the hikers reached Cold Spring Tunnel, they were greeted by cabins and tents, stacks of supplies and equipment, horses, mules, rail tracks, stores of dynamite, and piles of rubble from the excavation.

"No one can realize," wrote the reporter, "until they have seen for themselves, the amount of discomfort and hardship and even danger in which the men who are endeavoring to give Santa Barbara an adequate water supply work. Breathing

In the early 1980s, the Los Padres Forest Association organized volunteers to help maintain local trails. Volunteers gathered for work on the trail include (left to right) Connie Styrwol, Bob Burtness, two unidentified women, Jim Blakley, Vivian Obern, Sam Alfano, and U.S. Forest Service ranger, Jeff Saley. (Jim Blakley Collection, SBHM)

the foul air; clothing, from head to foot, saturated and dripping with muddy, cold water; suffering agony, with eyes blood-shot and inflamed, until one wonders if nature can completely restore or if the eyes may not be permanently injured….

"Neither may the horses be said to have an easy time. We met one laborious animal ascending the trail with a bale of hay strapped on either side, and it must be remembered that his is the only means of getting supplies to the camp, including railroad iron and the lumber necessary to support insecure places in the tunnel walls."

The dangers of working in the tunnels should have come as no surprise. In February, a *Morning Press* headline had blazed, "A SECOND TRAGEDY, Lang Ong, the Chinese Cook, Meets a Sudden Death." During a tremendous downpour at the end of January, an enormous boulder had thundered down the hillside and demolished the storage shed in which the cook was sleeping. The astonished reporter wrote, "His head was severed and the body fearfully mangled."

The very next month, the *Morning Press* reported another landslide had covered the entire entrance to the city tunnel, though no one was injured. Another time, gas temporarily blinded one of the workers there. The local papers continued to report on mishaps at this tunnel until 1903, when it was finally complete and soon to be obsolete. Nevertheless, at a bend in the trail, one can still find the concrete-faced adit of Cold Spring Tunnel looking very much like the entrance to a gated mausoleum, a testament to an era long gone.

#992

Hikers and riders were requested to close the gate at the entrance to La Cumbre Trail. La Cumbre, Spanish for "the peak," rises in the background, and the sign directs hikers to other adventures along Mountain Drive and Mission Canyon. (Stewart Edward White Collection, SBHM)

Reaching for La Cumbre

The early 1920s found Santa Barbarans sporting fashionable gear for exploring the front country.

Scorching sun, angry winds, and torrential rains have long since turned the wooden signs to dust and eroded the sandstone inscriptions along the once-famous La Cumbre Trail. Funded by the Santa Barbara Chamber of Commerce in 1902, the trail was the pride of the city, which boasted that only the tourist who had "explored her bewitching cañons and climbed her rugged mountains" could claim to have seen her grandest attractions.

Santa Barbarans cherished their trails, and families often spent two to four weeks camping in the mountains. Early newspapers reported on countless excursions and picnics in the bucolic canyons and on the rocky knolls. John Muir voiced the sentiments of these lovers of nature when he said, "Climb the mountains and get their tidings. Nature's peace will flow into you as sunshine flows into flowers and trees. The winds will blow their own freshness into you, and the storms their energy, while cares will drop like autumn leaves."

Riders and hikers wishing to find solace at the pinnacle of the range overlooking the coast, found the trail to be steep, subject to washouts, and in bad shape. In January 1902, the Chamber of Commerce started planning to move the trail westward so it would follow the ridge between Cold Spring Canyon and Rattlesnake Canyon.

In building the trail, the Chamber was continuing a tradition of trail stewardship that had started long before the creation of the forest reserve system in Santa Barbara. In April 1886, for instance, a group of young people had hosted an evening's entertainment consisting of poetry, music and song to benefit the Trail Fund.

The Chamber of Commerce Trail

Supporters of the La Cumbre Trail (aka the Chamber of Commerce Trail) had big plans. "Someday," reported the *Morning Press*, "there will be an easy wagon road leading up to La Cumbra [sic], to accommodate vehicles and automobiles; and it is quite within the range of possibilities that a trolley-line may be constructed to the place, getting its motive power from the Mission Cañon falls." Though the water-powered funicular never materialized, the Chamber did prepare for the future by securing a 40-foot wide right of way from property owners along the route.

As 1902 progressed, forest rangers did the work of surveying and clearing a two and one-half foot wide trail. Keeping a potential wagon road in mind, its grade was a gentle 6% to 8%. Trail committee members, E.S. Sheffield, Walter Hawley, and C.E. Edwards, alternated spending part of each day at the construction site, and, it was rumored, were not above rolling up their sleeves and pitching in on the work.

A party of hikers, alpenstocks in hand, pauses to admire the view from the Sentinel of the Abyss, aka Gibraltar Rock.

Riders dismounted to walk their horses on a narrow part of the trail in the 1920s.

By March, part of the new trail was clearly visible from the city below.

Another committee was formed to name the scenic points along the trail. By 1906 a Chamber of Commerce brochure urged visitors to catch their first glimpse of Montecito from *El Contento* and enjoy the views of Mission Canyon and Goleta from *El Reposo*. A large boulder at 1700 feet with steps carved into it was called *La Roca Grande*. (Later this rock was

Hikers take in spectacular views of the city and channel from atop La Roca Grande. Steps were carved into the rock and a chain handrail helped hikers reach the top safely.

called Inspiration Point.) Today's Gibraltar or Climbing Rock received the grand name of *La Centinela del Abysmo*.

Edward Selden Spaulding, an avid hiker of Rattlesnake Canyon, was not impressed with the hoopla surrounding the new La Cumbre Trail. "Things being what they were," he wrote in his memoirs, "it was inevitable that the high points would be designated with the usual touristy names." Regarding the "Sentinel of the Abyss," Spaulding wrote, "We boys could but speculate on which one of the 'backeasters' just come to town had thought up that silly, medieval designation."

He was also not alone in objecting to the change in name of nearby Rattlesnake Canyon to *Las Canoas*. Locals never accepted the new moniker, and mapmakers were inconsistent in labeling it. In 1905, the Chamber of Commerce capitulated and reverted back to the original name, mitigating its implied threat by proclaiming, "Not to the presence of rattlesnakes does the canyon owe its name, but alone to its slim sinuosity."

On George Washington's birthday in 1904, patriotic celebrants hoisted a giant flag on La Cumbre Peak, insuring that the pinnacle now reached 4,000 feet.

Celebrating La Cumbre

As the trail neared completion, promoters developed elaborate plans for a formal opening. One enthusiastic society matron even tried to recruit a couple to be married at the peak. The Age of Aquarius being still 60 years away, there were no takers.

On September 9, 1902, about 70 horsemen and women gathered at the Santa Barbara Mission for the trek along the new trail and the opening ceremony. Upon reaching a spring, they dismounted and spread blankets for a picnic repast, probably near Flores Flats, José Flores' homestead, which would soon to be dubbed *El Descanso*.

Sated and rested, the group continued to the summit and then eastward along the Ridge Trail to La Cumbre, the highest peak in the Santa Ynez range at 3,985 feet. Welcome

and commemorative speeches included an address on the commercial, spiritual, and healthful advantages of the trail by Reverend Warren D. More. The Horned Owl Quartette blew rousing tunes, the flag was raised, and Mrs. Walter C. Show (Alice Huse) sang "The Star Spangled Banner." A barbershop quartette sang "Drink to Me Only With Thine Eyes," and all joined in to sing "My Country 'Tis of Thee." As the sun lowered in the sky, the group wended their way homeward, enjoying the sublime and unparalleled splendor of the views along the trail.

The trail was enormously popular. In 1904, a patriotic group of 75 equestrians rode up on George Washington's birthday to plant a flag on the peak. Not just any flag, but a giant canvas American flag and a 30-foot staff that was carried up the trail in two pieces. Twenty previous trips had been made to drill a posthole in the rock for the staff and to bring up the cement and guide wires to secure it in place.

Flores Flats

A hardy trio admires the view from La Cumbre Peak, circa 1915.

One half-mile north of Rattlesnake Trail's junction with the La Cumbre Trail was Flores Flats. In 1900, José Flores had patented a homestead on the gently sloping hills and built a small redwood cabin below two tiny, permanent streams. He and his family had occupied the quarter section of land (160 acres) since 1895 and had improved the claim with an irrigation system consisting of a water flume and pipes, fencing, and a corral. He cultivated a vegetable garden, installed a vineyard, planted an orchard, and did a little trapping. "His catch was not large," wrote Edward Seldon Spaulding, "and what pelts he took were of poor quality; the ubiquitous skunk was his chief victim."

When the new trail opened, the enterprising Flores trapped tourists with a different bait: soda pop, which he cooled in a shaded pool and sold to the hot and dusty excursionists who rode by his house. Spaulding later wrote, "We boys, after the steep, hot climb to the Flats, found this soda pop to be altogether delicious."

A horseback party gathers at the summit of La Cumbre Peak soon after the trail opened. Arrows point to Arnold and Ida Eschenburg, a retired attorny and his daughter.

From the meadow near the top of Rattlesnake Canyon, hikers could reach La Cumbre Trail and Flores Flat.

Although Rattlesnake was Spaulding's preferred hiking trail, he and his friends often took La Cumbre Trail back to town. "It was fun to run much of the way and, by so doing, see how quickly we could make the six or seven mile journey."

The Trail Becomes a Road

After 1923 a fire lookout was placed on the peak. So popular was this site that visiting hours were instituted so the lookout in his glass house could undress in privacy and get some sleep. (In 1945, the U.S. Forest Service built a taller lookout station next to the old one, which was eventually removed.) During the 1920s, however, with Romero, Cold Spring, La Cumbre, Tunnel, and Arroyo Burro trails as well as San Marcos Pass leading to the ridge of the mountains, La Cumbre trail fell out of favor. Soon the chaparral and

In 1945, the forest service built a taller lookout next to the old one.

manzanita began to reclaim what was once theirs.

As unemployment and bank failures swept the nation during the 1930s, an alphabet soup of local, state, and federal relief agencies found ways to put men to work. Thanks to the county's unemployment relief plan, the mountain wall was to see three trails become roads: Romero, La Cumbre, and the Ridge Trail, which became Camino Cielo. Under the auspices of the State Emergency Relief Administration, men working with picks, shovels, compressors, and dynamite scraped a road over the old La Cumbre trail, deviating at times from its path.

Finally, the original plan for a road was in place, but its romantic Spanish name devolved into "Depression Avenue." The citizenry strongly objected to this new moniker, so in 1933 the road was renamed Gibraltar Road, since it was to

The peak's first fire lookout station was errected in 1923.

continue down the north slope to reach the dam of the same name. By 1937, local social club Los Rancheros Visitadores was using the road to reach the *Juan y Lolita*, the Mitchell Ranch, for their annual "Ride."

As with the trail, nature continually tries to reclaim this road, which is prone to rock and mud slides. Though its disintegrating surface is at times rough and pockmarked, it still, as a 1906 Chamber of Commerce brochure claimed, "… runs along the walls of canyons, over lofty spurs, across picturesque ridges, through groves of pines, till coming to that mighty rock (La Cumbre) where one stands between heaven and earth and the beholder is awed into silence by the vastness of the landscape."

The State Emergency Relief Administration fulfilled the dreams of the 1902 Chamber of Commerce and reconstructed the trail as a road in the 1930s. Santa Barbarans weren't having the new name of Depression Drive, however, and quickly renamed it Gibraltar Road. (SERA photo album, SBHM)

During the 1890s, patrons of Santa Barbara's Hot Springs Resort could choose to rent a room in the hotel or pitch a tent.

Montecito's Hot Springs Canyon

By 1880, Montecito's hot springs were so ancient that the *Morning Press* felt compelled to write their history. The hot springs, the article said, had been used by the Chumash tribes since time immemorial. After the arrival of the Europeans, the springs, though belonging first to the Pueblo and then to the City of Santa Barbara, "were preserved for the use of the citizens who chose to take benefit of their healing properties, or for thrifty washerwomen." In fact, whole families used to camp near the springs for several days while the women pounded the dirt out of that season's laundry and laid the items over accommodating bushes to dry.

During California's Mexican period (1821 to 1848), foreigners were allowed to trade in Santa Barbara, and a brisk hide and tallow business developed. In 1829, Alfred Robinson, an agent for the Boston-based company of Bryant & Sturgis, set up shop in Santa Barbara. In his memoir, Robinson described a visit to the springs.

"We rode across the little settlement of Montecito," he wrote, "and soon came to a rough and narrow passage leading to the mountains, which we ascended till the path became so intricate that it was impossible to proceed further on horseback; so … we walked to the spring, where the waters were boiling up with much force. There are a few shanties on the spot for the accommodation of families, who frequently pass several days there during the summer months."

When Private Walter Murray arrived in Santa Barbara as a member of Company F of the First New York Volunteer Infantry in April 1847, he was placed on garrison duty and had plenty of free time to reconnoiter the area. In his memoir he wrote, "One of our favorite resorts was the Sulphur or hot springs." After negotiating the overgrown trail, Murry wrote

The 1881 Morning Press *advertisement for the hot springs says a stage can take guests there or sulphur water can be delivered to one's home.*

that his companions had found "three or four springs of differing temperatures and different ingredients, if one may judge by the color; one of them being a bright pinkish hue, another green, another indistinguishable from ordinary water."

Glowing reports from early travelers of the efficacy of the springs induced Wilbur Curtiss to construct a resort, which would grow to include several outbuildings.

In later years, studies revealed some 20-plus springs ranging in temperature from 60 degrees to 120 degrees Fahrenheit. The medicinal properties of these springs were believed to be of great value in treating a multitude of diseases.

Medical scientists of the time asserted that rheumatism, gout, Bright's disease, liver troubles, and bladder irritation were sure to disappear with daily treatments of the spa waters. The antacid quality of the water benefited dyspepsia and conditions of the blood and urine. In addition, syphilitic and scrofulous contaminations and chronic skin diseases greatly benefited from bathing in the salubrious liquids.

Murray reported that each spring flowed into a natural basin in which he and his friends used to immerse themselves. "These springs," he wrote, "would make the fortune of any town in the United States but here are left alone and deserted, visited alone by the native sick or the American sojourner in Santa Barbara."

Development

In 1855, Wilbur Curtiss, whose health was broken after years of mining, arrived in Santa Barbara and was shown the springs, which worked a miracle on his ailments. As his health improved, he envisioned a lucrative future for himself as owner and operator of a thriving health resort. Much to the dismay of the 1880s reporter, Curtiss made a preemption claim and set about making improvements. He started with tents, then huts, then cottages, and then a hotel. He also built an access road to the resort.

Curtiss (right) sought to make his fortune from the springs that cured his ailments, but Mother Nature had other ideas.

In the 1890s Edwin H. Sawyer, owner of the Hot Springs Resort, leased it out to a variety of proprietors. Jennie A. Kimberly (black hat and dress)

took charge of the resort for several years.

Redwood flumes moved the hot springs waters to the bathhouses.

to find investors for the construction of a hotel at the mouth of the canyon to which he planned to pipe spring waters. His prospectus promoted a lodge with 46 bedrooms, many with private bathrooms and sitting rooms. Unfortunately, investors failed to materialize.

In 1871, wildfire destroyed all of Curtiss' buildings in the canyon. It took years to rebuild and he went into debt. In 1877, his property was sold in a foreclosure sale after which a succession of owners and managers tried their hands at running the enterprise. In 1886, at the height of the California land boom, Montecito landowner Edwin H. Sawyer bought the resort and its attendant 320 acres as an investment. When the boom went bust the following year, he tried to interest others to manage or buy the resort, but somehow the property kept returning to his possession.

Testimonial

*I*n 1885, Katherine E. Payne of Massachusetts was visiting friends in Santa Barbara and was introduced to a handsome young lawyer named James William Taggart. Will introduced her to the Hot Springs where together with friend Lillie Calkins, they lunched, bathed, and hiked to the popular Lookout Point. Katie returned home much inspired by her visit.

By June, Katie was suffering from mysterious headaches. Her doctor prescribed several weeks of treatments at the Sulphur Springs Resort in Montecito. After a morning sulphur bath and hike at the resort, Katie was treated to mud packs, arsenic drinks and arsenic baths in the afternoon. In the evenings, guests gathered in the parlor where Katie joined in the entertainment by playing guitar. On the Fourth of July, guests marched to the halfway house accompanied by Katie's patriotic tunes played on paper and comb. Later they watched the fireworks and rockets sent skyward from the city below.

Curtiss's health may have improved by his association with the springs, but his fortune didn't. The road was subject to washouts in heavy rains, and in the winter of 1861/62, one of the men living in a canvas shanty at the springs was killed by a landslide. Realizing the difficulty and perils of operating a resort in such a remote and precarious site, Curtiss decided

During the 1880s, Katherine E. Payne found more than just her health at the Hot Springs.

A mule-drawn sled helps an invalided guest to the bath house for a cure.

During this time, Katie renewed her acquaintance with Will Taggart, who was destined to become a noted California judge. The hot springs did their work; Katie's ailments disappeared and the two married in 1887. Years later, when their daughter was ill, they obtained permission to take her to the then closed Hot Springs Resort. There, they found the hotel occupied by a colony of rats, so each night the caretaker sat in the rafters spearing rodents, bagging 40 to 50 each night. At the end of their stay, their young daughter, who had somehow survived drinking a multitude of glasses of sulfur and arsenic water, was proclaimed well.

Canyon Trials and Tribulations

Fire and rain were constant threats to the resort. In 1889, for instance, heavy rains sent a boulder tumbling that demolished three sides of a bathhouse occupied only moments before by the children of Reverend P. S. Thacher. Mountain lions and coyotes decimated hotel livestock, and downstream riparian owners objected to people with scrofulous complaints bathing in their drinking water.

In 1905, Edwin Sawyer was finally relieved of his white elephant when a group of investors bought the property. Once again, talk of a hotel at the mouth of the canyon surfaced. Once again, nothing came of it. In 1910, W. H. Bartlett and S.P. Calef, neighbors on Middle Road in Montecito, bought the resort, and in 1914 they organized the Hot Springs Club, for the purpose of enjoying the waters of the springs. Initially, the exclusive club was comprised of only 15 members.

In 1921, fire destroyed the old hotel building and a new clubhouse was built on its stone foundations. Eventually the

Picnickers, like this musical and romantic group, found the Hot Spring Canyon hike to be an idyllic outing, but the owners of the resort complained that they spent no money.

Guests gathered on the precariously perched porch of the Hot Springs Hotel for this stereopticon.

The Hot Springs Club in the 1920s or '30s

owners dried up when trespassers broke the pipelines of the Montecito Creek Water Company to fill makeshift tarp-lined spas and built campfires in the fire-prone canyon. One man went so far as to dam the creek, build a cement-and-tile spa, and hand out business cards with a toll-free number.

When the owners of the 462-acre canyon property wanted to sell, the Land Trust for Santa Barbara County launched a successful capital campaign and purchased it in 2012. The Trust then spent another 19 months working with government agencies, utility companies, and neighboring owners before being able to transfer the deed to the United States Forest Service, thereby returning Montecito's Hot Springs Trail to public ownership. The 1880s *Morning Press* reporter, who had bemoaned the public's loss of the historic hot springs, would have been pleased.

clubhouse fell into disuse, and Kenneth Hunter, Sr. with Larry McCaslin acquired the property in 1962, purchasing the shares of the Club owners. Hunter repaired the building and made improvements only to have the devastating Coyote Fire of 1964 turn his enterprise to ashes. In 1986, Kenneth Hunter, Jr. sold his shares of the land to McCaslin Properties which planned to develop the acreage.

Hikers had been using the Hot Springs Trail for centuries. The 1904 *Guide to Rides and Drives in Santa Barbara and Vicinity* promoted the springs and the view from Lookout Point. The Hikers, a club founded in 1913, held their inaugural outing on January 11, 1914, with a hike up Cold Spring Trail and down Hot Springs Trail. Nevertheless, ever since Wilbur Curtiss was given his certificate of purchase to the land in 1870, hikers had been traversing private property.

Owners of the hotel, restaurant and spa in the 1880s had complained about picnickers who used the land and spent no money. A hundred years later, the tolerance of the property

The Coyote Fire of 1964 destroyed the clubhouse and opened the door to potential suburban development of the canyon.

The Dinsmore family—Agnes on the white horse, Tom wearing a badge, and Gus leading a pack horse—along with an unidentified man, leave Montecito via the Romero Trail, circa 1910. (Montecito Association History Committee — MAHiC)

Up and Over Romero Canyon

Romero Canyon Trail in Montecito climbs steadily toward magnificent views from the crest of the mountain before plunging into Blue Canyon and continuing down to the Santa Ynez River. In the beginning, the Chumash Indians of Montecito's Salaguas village used the canyon path to obtain food in the Santa Ynez Valley and to trade with the villages of the interior. Later, Californios used the trail as a means of reaching the headquarters of Rancho de Los Prietos y Najalayegua and the upper Santa Ynez River.

During the American period, years of disuse allowed nature to reclaim the trail until the late 1850s, when it was recut as a dispatch route to carry mail to Fort Tejon. The route was never used, however, so rain and neglect once again reduced it to a terrible condition.

In 1861, explorer and writer William H. Brewer hired a guide to lead his party over the Romero Canyon Trail. Brewer wrote, "Such a trail as we found that day! The worst I had traveled before was a turnpike compared with that. Now following along a narrow ledge, now in the brook over boulders, now dismounting and jumping our mules over logs, or urging them to mount rocks I would have believed inaccessible–yet this was 'pretty good yet' our guide told us."

In 1903, Rancho de Los Prietos y Najalayegua became part of the forest reserve system that was intended to preserve the watershed lands of the Santa Ynez River. In 1908, four local reserves merged to form Santa Barbara National Forest, and in 1938, as reserves from farther afield joined the system, the name changed to Los Padres National Forest. Through it all, the Romero Trail continued to be a main route into the backcountry as Montecitans and Santa Barbarans took to the hills to work the mines, grow the pines, graze their cattle, and hunt deer or simply fish, camp and be at one with nature.

Early Romero Canyon Dwellers

Montecito was settled primarily by descendents of Presidio soldiers, and none were greater in number than the Romero clan. They occupied enclaves in Spanish Town at the foot of Parra Grande Lane, on Cota Lane, and on Romero Hill, which lay east of today's Miramonte Lane. By the 1870s, brothers Mariano and Apolinario had joined other Romeros in claiming most of the lands along San Ysidro Creek. In 1880 and 1891, respectively, Apolinario and Mariano received patents for homesteads in Romero Canyon as well.

Mariano and his second wife, Catarina (Kate) Vogelmann Romero, built a four-room house in the canyon and planted grapevines and fruit trees, mostly oranges and apples. Their children rode horseback to the Ortega School (1889-1922), located on East Valley Road at the base of Romero Canyon Road.

Romero Canyon Road ended at Romo Flats where a one-room shack served as the solitary abode of a Mr. Romo. Romo had also planted grapes and citrus, which he watered via a dirt irrigation ditch leading from a spring on his land. His wife, being afraid of rattlesnakes and other wild animals, declined to live with him.

In 1906, the John B. Cottam family moved from New

Mariano Romero and his wife Kate (Jacobine Catarina Vogelmann) owned a homestead in Romero Canyon. (Raymond B. Romero Collection, Montecito Association History Committee)

In 1915, Jose del Carmen Romero, owner of the Montecito Livery stable, escorted Grace Meeker and Isabelle Baker, visitors and later residents, on many excursions into the mountains. (Baker Family Album; MAHiC)

Jersey to Tabor Lane in Montecito and established a farm and apiary. The two Cottam boys attended the Ortega School and made many forays into the backcountry via nearby Romero Trail.

In 1912, 14-year-old Albert Cottam was invited to spend a few weeks with an elderly Mr. Chard who lived in the Pendola adobe on the Santa Ynez River. Albert saddled his horse Ruskie–so named because Albert's father had bought

the horse off a Russian cowboy from Salinas–and rode over the Romero Trail to meet Chard, who regaled him with tales of the early days of Montecito and Romero Canyon. Chard claimed to have known the infamous bandit, Joaquin Murietta, and he showed Albert many documents and drawings, some signed by the Mexican governor of California and the president of Mexico.

Chard told Albert that in the late 1800s, about a mile up

Students from Ortega School, which stood on East Valley Road near Sheffield Road across from Romero Canyon, pose with their teacher for a group photo circa 1913. Among those pictured are 1. Miss Molly Brown (teacher); 5. Ray B. Romero; 8. Albert Cottam; and 11. Warren Cottam. (Raymond B. Romero Collection, Montecito Association History Committee)

Romero Road, there was an Indian cave. "In this cave," Albert related in a 1975 interview, "lived an old hermit and a young boy around 15 years old whom the hermit had kidnapped. He used this boy to run errands like stealing food and other items. The last trip the boy made, he was caught and shot to death and was buried in an olive grove on Jackson's old place" [the San Carlos Ranch].

Beyond the cave, Cottam remembered old horses were shot and put to rest in a side canyon, which became known as Horse Canyon. Sulfur springs dotted the creek, and Ralph Whitehead's water tunnel tapped into the fresh water retained in the mountain sandstone. (Whitehead was the original creator of the *Arcady* estate in Montecito, which was purchased by George Owen Knapp in 1911.)

Gus (left) and Tom Dinsmore cut hay at Mono Flats along the Santa Ynez River. (Cogan/Dinsmore Collection, MAHiC)

Fred Forbush's homestead cabin where he planted apple trees and was a neighbor of the Cottams and Shows. (E.R. "Jim" Blakley Collection, SBHM)

Wilderness Camps

In 1915, Albert Cottam and his older brother Russell built a cabin and established a camp in the meadow near the end of Blue Canyon. Pack mules trudged up Romero Canyon loaded with four-foot boards to cover a frame of alder poles. The brothers brought wealthy clients into the meadow, cooking for them and caring for them. They also harvested hay for their pack animals. Albert often packed in U.S. Forest Service workers who set up spike camps far in the backcountry. He returned to them twice a week carrying fresh meat, mail, and newspapers.

The Cottams' closest neighbor on the other side of the mountain lived two miles west at the head of Forbush Canyon, where homesteader Fred Forbush had built a cabin and planted a small apple orchard. In 1926, the Cottams acquired another neighbor. Herbert "Dad" Show and his son, Roderick Show, established Camp Ynez a quarter mile west of the Cottams.

Herbert was the nephew of Walter Show of the famous grocery firm, Show and Hunt. He had opened the first local poultry ranch off San Leandro Lane in Montecito. Herbert and his son built a small-scale guest ranch composed mainly of tents. "Dad" Show was chaperone, cook, and wrangler for many groups of young people who stayed at the camp. Herbert later worked for the forest service and was superintendent at Los Prietos Ranger Station.

Another group of Romero Canyon dwellers was the family of Tom Dinsmore, the grandson of Colonel Bradbury True Dinsmore, who had brought his extended family to farm in Montecito in 1867. Tom worked on a ranch in Romero Canyon for a time. He, and later his son Gus, hired on with the forest service. The Dinsmores often rode over Romero Canyon and into the backcountry to camp, fish, and hunt in addition to performing forest service work such as planting

In 1915, Russell Cottam leads his horse away from the framework for the hayrick at their wilderness camp at the junction of Blue and Forbush canyons. (E.R. "Jim" Blakley Collection, SBHM)

Wilderness guide Russell Cottam with deer he bagged in the Big Pine/ Madulce area of the Santa Barbara backcountry, circa 1920. (E.R. "Jim" Blakley Collection, SBHM)

pines, constructing and maintaining trails and fighting fires. They were stationed for several years at a log cabin at Madulce before moving to the Santa Ynez River at Mono Creek, where they constructed an adobe.

Like Albert Cottam, a young Tom Dinsmore also met the old man staying at the Pendola adobe. Mr. Chard had invited him for dinner, and when Tom rode into the ranch, the old man was waiting with a particular treat. A deer's head he had

Warren Cottam on Gladys at Cottam's Cabin at the end of Blue Canyon (E.R. "Jim" Blakley Collection, SBHM)

Rod and Herbert Show, seen here circa 1926, opened Camp Ynez at the mouth of Forbush Canyon. (E.R. "Jim" Blakley Collection, SBHM)

cooked for the young lad sat in the middle of the table with the eyes still in it. As Tom sat down to table, the old man reached over with a stick, gouged out an eye, and popped it into his mouth. Aghast, Tom levitated out of his chair and flew out the screen door. He politely declined all future invitations to dine with Mr. Chard.

A Road Comes and Goes

Romero Canyon changed drastically after 1933. After Juncal Dam was completed in 1930, the Civilian Conservation Corps bulldozed a road over the mountain to provide access. Traversed for many years, the road fell into disuse in the late 1960s and has not been regularly maintained.

Santa Barbara businessman and member of Los Rancheros Visitadores, James "Jim" Andros, had been active in the Santa Barbara backcountry for many years. As a young man he drove Romero Canyon Road many times to get to his properties in the wilderness. In the 1970s, Jim and two partners purchased 490 acres of Romero Canyon for $90,000.

In 1978, concerned that so many of Montecito's canyons

The Dinsmores were stationed for a time at the Madulce Cabin. Hazel Dinsmore, Tom Dinsmore, and a Mr. Wood chat in the outdoor kitchen. Bread has just been baked in the Dutch oven in the foreground. (Cogan/ Dinsmore Collection, MAHiC)

Jim Andros riding a Santa Barbara trail on "Nugget"

were sprouting houses and development, the trio, comprised of Jim Andros, Joseph Zebrosky and Dr. Glen Counihan, offered to sell Romero Canyon to the Trust for Public Land for the price they had paid plus a $30,000 tax credit. They stipulated that the land was never to be built upon. The Trust held the land until the U.S. Forest Service could purchase it in 1980.

Thanks to the generosity of these three men, Romero Canyon remains in its relatively native state. Today, the forces of nature, rather than urban development, determine its changing character.

(top) Camp in Blue Canyon in 1905, complete with cookbook and coyote (middle) Corral and outbuildings at Pendola Ranch (bottom) The Pendola adobe, circa 1911, where Mr. Chard entertained Albert Cottam and Tom Dinsmore many years earlier (E.R. "Jim" Blakley collection, SBHM)

A carreta leaves the Santa Barbara Mission in Alexander Harmer's painting of Spanish days in Santa Barbara.
(Courtesy Louise Clarke and John Carbon)

Section Three

Wheeled Revolution

❧✦❧

The Spanish introduced wheeled vehicles to Santa Barbara in the form of the carreta, a crude two-wheeled cart with spokeless wooden wheels. In the early days of Spanish colonization of Santa Barbara (initiated in 1782 for the Presidio and 1786 for the Mission), they were the mainstay for transportation of crops, goods and people. Drawn by oxen, carretas provided a bone-rattling ride accompanied by the screech of ungreased wheels. Legend has it that the screech was tolerated because it warded off evil spirits that lay in wait along the caminos.

Spanish Santa Barbara became Mexican Santa Barbara in 1821 after the 11-year war for independence from Spain. A scant 17 years later, Mexican California became American California after the conclusion of the Mexican American War in 1848.

In these early days, ships and horses were the preferred method of transportation for traveling outside the area. It wasn't until 1861 that stage service was instituted between San Francisco and Santa Barbara. After the completion of the Chapala Street Wharf in 1869 and Stearns Wharf in 1872, however, most people chose to travel to Los Angeles and San Francisco by boat. They preferred the relative ease of travel over water to the lurching of stages on dusty, muddy, and jarring roadways.

In the late 1800s two wheels became popular as intrepid Santa Barbara wheelmen and women took to the streets on their bicycles, often frightening horses and pedestrians alike. These cyclists became the first to agitate for improved roadways.

Then in 1887, the railroad reached Santa Barbara from Los Angeles. Since the coastal road between Carpinteria and Ventura had been narrowed to accommodate the tracks, most stages and wagons now used the Casitas Pass. Others watched the tide tables carefully before venturing along that stretch of coast.

In 1901, when the rail line between Santa Barbara to San Francisco had finally connected and passenger service became available, Wells Fargo drove its last stage over San Marcos Pass. However, even as Santa Barbarans celebrated the completion of the Coast Line, the harbinger of its decline was already on the road. In March of 1901, a Locomobile carrying Mr. and Mrs. George W. Beauhoff of Philadelphia completed a 3,000-mile coast-to-coast trip and surmounted San Marcos Pass to alight in Santa Barbara.

Inspired by the enormous public interest an automobile on State Street had elicited, W.S. Sherman of Santa Barbara bought a mail order Locosurrey in September of that year and operated it as a rental machine. It was garaged at Short's Bicycle Shop at 718 State Street. He charged $15 round trip to the mission, including use of duster and goggles.

By 1909 there were nearly 300 horseless carriages in Santa Barbara, and the stage was set for a revolution in both transportation and lifestyle.

In 1888, the Ventura Wheelmen Club cycled to Santa Barbara where they posed on State Street with their safety bicycles.

Santa Barbara on Two Wheels

Looking neat, upon the seats of a bicycle built for two, a duo of Italian wheelmen rolled into Santa Barbara on May 10, 1901. Carlo Reiter and Mino Galvini had left Florence, Italy, on July 5, 1899, after members of their biking club wagered 50,000 francs that they couldn't ride 75,000 miles by Christmas Day 1902.

Though the two rode as representatives of the Florence *Courier* and Milan *Sporting Life*, they had to cover their expenses en route through lectures, wrestling and fencing exhibitions, and photography sales. They carried with them an

Intended to promote the national movement for good roads, this photo shows the consequences of "normal" road conditions on American cyclists.
(Library of Congress)

album filled with autographs of all the mayors of the towns they had visited as well as the governors of the states.

The Italian globe-trotters planned to write a book about their travels and live in affluence off the profits. The *Morning Press* could not refrain from remarking, "…Both men are splendid examples of manhood."

They were certainly not the first tourists to pass through town on a bicycle. Wheelmen from Ventura and Carpinteria visited regularly. In 1891, Alex S. Gardiner of San Francisco, enthralled by California's landscape, took 10 days to meander down to Santa Barbara. The *Santa Barbara Independent* wrote that he arrived "with a well-tanned face and a splendid appetite."

Although the automobile would become the preferred method of wheeled transportation by 1910, it was the bicycle that initiated the Good Roads Movement in the United States. In 1880, bicycle enthusiasts, riding clubs, and bicycle manufacturers met in Rhode Island to form the League of American Wheelmen. They became a national organization in 1891 and a major force for improved roads.

In 1892, an impassioned editorial in the *Morning Press* lobbied for better roads to bring out the true efficiency of the bicycle as a form of transportation. In 1897, the California legislature authorized the creation of bicycle lanes and paths, so the Wheelmen of Santa Barbara circulated a petition to create a bicycle path leading from Santa Barbara to Carpinteria.

By 1901, however, the roads were not much improved, so one enterprising San Francisco wheelman decided to avoid them altogether. He modified his bicycle wheels to ride one rail, adding an outrigger-style flange for support from the other. He first rode south along the Central Valley line, covering 500 miles in 2½ days. Then, taking advantage of the recently completed Coast Line, he cruised through Santa Barbara in April.

The Bicycle Craze

The bicycle had taken Santa Barbara by storm by the 1880s, and in 1885 the *Morning Press* reported, "Bicycle riding has become more than a fad or popular pastime; it is a craze. Everybody rides, grandmothers, children, businessmen, ministers, society women." Stables became concerned when their businesses declined, and one wag said that local horses had tears in their eyes when Dixie Thompson, renowned host of the Arlington Hotel and avid equestrian, tried out a high wheeler.

The switch from high wheelers to safety bicycles with equally sized wheels, pneumatic tires and chain or shaft drives, as well as the use of mass production techniques that brought the price down, had a tremendous impact on the popularity of the bicycle. The Pope Manufacturing Company, maker of Columbia bicycles, sold 200,000 bicycles in 1889 and one million in 1899.

The bicycle's popularity led to a plethora of bicycle-related inventions. In the third quarter of 1896 alone, the U.S. Patent Office received applications for more than 1,000 of these devices. While the majority dealt with the mechanics of the bike–tires, brakes, chains, etc.–others dealt with the convenience of the rider. There were 14 applications for devices to secure women's dresses, seven for bells, two devices for carrying pipes and matches, two for "toilette companions," and one bicycling gourmand pitched a contrivance for carrying luncheons.

In Santa Barbara, a Professor Morse was experimenting with inflating tires with various gases, but most destroyed

PUCK Magazine's *take on the "New Woman" of the 1890s reveals the liberating effects of the "freedom machine." (Library of Congress)*

A woman cyclist wears liberating shirtwaist attire while peddling along a local street. (Stewart Edward White Collection; SBHM)

High wheeled bicycles had the advantage of a faster and smoother ride, but the safety bicycles appealed to a greater number of people. This intrepid trio was photographed in Isaac N. Cook's Santa Barbara studio about 1885.

the rubber in a few days. When he tried hydrogen it reduced the weight by eight pounds. He claimed that with aluminum frames and a mixture of oxygen and hydrogen gas, a bicycle could weigh under 10 pounds.

Once the center bar was dropped, the bicycle became suitable for women. Susan B. Anthony, pioneer suffragette and feminist, called it the "freedom machine" and said, "… it has done more to emancipate women than anything else in the world." The bicycle craze also aided the movement for "rational dress" for women.

In an 1896 "Local Outing," the newsletter of Henry S. Short's Bicycle Supply House and Repair Shop, Charles Dudley Warren claimed it was "a landmark year for the progress of women and consequently the evolution of society." Warren, an American essayist, novelist, and editor of *Harper's*

Magazine, believed bicycling led to an outdoor life that would broaden a woman's life view, provide physical and mental health, and make her more cheerful and better prepared for her "duties of the day." (You know, like washing, ironing, fetching her husband's slippers. – Ah, Charles, and you started out so promising!)

Bicycles even invaded the nation's political life. Urged by the Republican National Committee, the Santa Barbara wheelmen held an illuminated parade to support William McKinley's 1896 bid for the presidency. The *Morning Press* reported, "There was a brilliant display of Japanese lanterns, red and blue lights, and the wheelmen went through many pretty maneuvers while going up and down State Street." The music of bicycle bells was supplemented by a chorus of tin horns.

Go Fast, Young Man

Put two men on two bicycles and there will be a race. By 1896, Santa Barbara wheelmen had their own bicycle race track. That year, the Floral Festival included amateur and professional races. Even the city's Chinese population got in on the act. The *Santa Barbara Independent* reported, "The mile Chinese race was an interesting one and four of our local Celestials took part. The contestants are well-known riders of the wheel and … appeared in regulation racing costume and humped themselves like professionals. Jim Fong was the winner with Yee Yeh second and Sam Wah third. Best time was 5:21."

In August 1894, Harry Mitchell had set the record for "rapid bicycling" over mountain roads in the Central Coast. He rode to Ventura, enjoyed a repast of meat and potatoes, raced a horse and rider to Nordhoff (Ojai), left them in the dust, and returned to Santa Barbara in four hours and 45 minutes. His $50 Waverley and he were none the worse for wear.

Unfortunately, the safety bicycle wasn't all that safe, and accidents–small and large–warranted press coverage. In 1894, the *Independent* reported, "There was a miscellaneous mixture of two Chinamen, two bicycles, and a small dog on Canon Perdido Street last evening."

Runaway horses trampled several bicyclists over the years. Carl Wood was run over by a runaway vegetable horse and cart in 1909 and knocked unconscious. On the other hand, also in 1909, Florence Baxter Eaton, wife of artist Charles Frederick Eaton, was seriously injured on State Street when she was knocked unconscious by a delivery boy on a bike. The wind had been blowing sand in his eyes and he did not see her.

While pedestrians usually ended up on the losing side of a bike encounter, the June 1896 *Morning Press* reported on one woman whom bicyclists just didn't run into. The reporter wrote, "One man did it and wasn't able to sit down for several

In addition to races, Santa Barbara wheelmen participated in the Floral parades of the 1890s. Here George Gourley (left) and friend won first prize in the novelty category for their sailboat suspended between their two bicycles.

days. He was going at a pretty fair gait along Chapala Street and ran into the above-mentioned woman. She did not wait to send a complaint to the council but just grabbed the young man by the nape of the neck, laid him across her knee and bore down heavy. As he crawled away with his wheel, she said, 'I let you off pretty easy this time, young fellow, but if you ever run into me again, you'll wish bicycles were never invented!'"

This rider, with his flower-encased bicycle, is ready for the floral parade.

(below) In 1899, author Stewart Edward White wrote, "Canfield and I took a long trip on bicycles through some of the more unfrequented parts of Brittany. In many places we were looked upon as curiosities." Attorney Robert B. Canfield lived in Santa Barbara and White would soon move there as well. (Stewart Edward White Collection; SBHM)

Santa Barbara had tried to tackle the safety problem in 1894 with various ordinances. Bicyclists were prohibited from riding in Plaza del Mar because, reported the *Morning Press,* "of the habit of reckless younger riders to speed about without regard to the rights of pedestrians and sightseers." Wheelmen were required to have bells, and it was suggested by one city council member that the type of bell be specified in order to prevent recalcitrant bicyclists from "carrying cow bells as a burlesque of the ordinance." By way of compensation, the council raised the speed limit from seven miles per hour to 10. Nevertheless, the wheelmen complained bitterly about the ordinance, saying bells startled pedestrians who jumped into the way of the bike. Many claimed they'd rather sell their wheels than obey such an absurd law.

In the 1920s, automobile touring stages took visitors through Sequoia and Yosemite National Parks.

Auto Touring and Camping

By the early part of the 20th century, Americans were putting their horses out to pasture and hitting the open road in their shiny automobiles. Despite early campaigns by America's wheelmen for improved roads, muddy conditions, steep ascents, and dangerous river crossings continued to plague wheeled vehicles. These were not the only hazards that motorists faced. Though travel by stagecoach was a thing of the past, highway robbery was not.

In July 1920, four automobile stages heading for Yosemite Valley were held up by a bandit wearing overalls, a miner's shirt, and a flour sack over his head. The outlaw had thrown a log across the road and hidden in the bushes. When the four

Before there was a bridge at the Gaviota Gorge, horse and wagon traffic had to ford the creek. No wonder automobiles would become stuck at various crossings during times of high water.

In the back seat, Sally Taylor Alexander (later Stow) with son Taylor and friends prepare to be ferried across the Santa Ynez River after their sojourn at Camp Alexander, circa 1912. (MAHiC)

caravanning auto stages stopped at the barrier, the masked man emerged brandishing a rifle and demanding wallets. The bandit's code of honor, however, prevented him from robbing two of the stages, which were filled with Boy Scouts from New York.

Closer to home, autoists traveling over a particularly bad stretch of road near Las Cruces cried "highway robbery" at the rates a local rancher charged to assist them in crossing Gaviota Creek where a bridge had washed out. Apparently, he was demanding as much as $20 to extricate stalled cars from the stream. The *Morning Press* reported, "So lucrative has the traffic become that he has kept a man and a team of horses at the crossing daily, waiting for unlucky tourists."

Promotion of Touring and Camping

*S*unset magazine, created by the Southern Pacific Railroad to entice Easterners west, recognized the potential of automobile travel early on. In 1903, the magazine recommended a four-day trip from San Francisco to Los Angeles. In 1913, the magazine published a series called "Autobirds of Passage" which was the record of a motor trip from Mexico to Alaska. In 1916, its pages offered "Practical Hints for Motor Camping."

The Automobile Club of America, meanwhile, started providing maps in 1906 and publishing a magazine, *Touring Topics*, in 1909. *Touring Topics* (which became *Westways*) not only gave motorists ideas for excursions but also promoted auto camping and its attendant paraphernalia through informative articles with titles like "For Nomads of the Open Road" and "Togs and Things for Campers."

One American humorist cited by the magazine claimed one could acquire all the sensations of camping merely by "sitting comfortably attired in one's own house with all the screens open, a willing prey to flies and mosquitoes, partaking of canned beans and coffee diluted with canned milk." Camping enthusiasts, however, couldn't wait to go "gypsying" and were on the hunt for the perfect camping accessories. American inventors and manufacturers were happy to oblige.

In a 1929 edition of *Touring Topics*, Opal Haynes

In 1913, Sunset Magazine's series, "Autobirds of Passage," the story of a road trip from Mexico to Alaska, stopped along Alameda Padre Serra to admire the Santa Barbara Mission.

recommended the Dickeybird-Kamper tent, which would "prove impenetrable to the most enterprising mosquito. Flies and insects of all sorts might as well not attempt to 'crash the gate' of this tent, for the netting door, which slides on a rope cable, and the six-inch sill are most discouraging to such intruders." The door even sprang shut automatically.

Tent furnishings ranged from 40-pound spring beds to 18-pound steel cots to down sleeping bags with detachable

Let's Eat **UTILITY AUTO KITCHENETTE**

"It's the Camper's Pet"

MANUFACTURED BY

RIDDLE SHEET METAL WORKS

1067-71 FOLSOM STREET   SAN FRANCISCO

The Utility Auto Kitchenette is a combined camping stove, oven, icebox and pantry—made of metal throughout. For the auto trip, on the yacht, for light housekeeping. There is a place for everything—it seals all contents tightly, keeping out dust, dirt and weather. It is built by a lover of the out-of-doors, who knows from experience the real needs of the camper. Carried on running board or trunk rack. Ask your Dealer or write for illustrated folder.

The May Co.   **J. Andrews & Co.**
Broadway at Eighth St.   1739 W. Pico St.
LOS ANGELES, CALIFORNIA

American manufacturers and advertisers were quick to capitalize on the motor camping craze.

Owners of horse-drawn excursion businesses retired the temperamental beasts and purchased motorized stages to take their clients to the summit of San Marcos Pass.

wool blankets. The latter was the choice of the seasoned camper who sometimes augmented the bag with a 4-pound silk air mattress. A radical alternative to the whole tent system was a Pullman conversion of the car, which allowed the seats to fold back into a bed, and camp cars, which sprouted tent wings.

No camp set up was complete without a folding

bathtub and table and chairs. For cooking essentials, Auto Kitchenettes included a two-burner stove, oven, insulated ice box, water bucket, gasoline tank, and cabinet for foodstuffs as well as a separate egg container. The whole kit packed up into a 12 inches x 23 inches x 35 inches rectangle and the opened door formed a table for four. For those who preferred individual pieces, the Stonebridge Folding Baker or Auto Cook Oven folded into small packages and guaranteed the camper hot biscuits, corn bread, baked potatoes, and even broiled meats. For cold water, the makers of a device called the Zeronator claimed it would cool water instantly without ice; it looked suspiciously like a cocktail shaker.

Folding chairs, folding canvas buckets, folding candle lanterns, folding pans, folding cots—they all were designed to stow neatly on the running boards of the camper's car.

The names of early manufacturers of camping equipment have mostly faded from our memories, but the Coleman company is still going strong after more than 100 years. Founded by W.C. Coleman in 1901, the company originally

Flappers rejoiced in the freedom of the automobile for camping and picnic excursions. This local Santa Barbara lass smiles from a running board loaded with picnic paraphernalia.

sold lanterns to rural areas where electricity was unavailable or unreliable. Though Coleman did not invent the Efficient Lamp, which operated by pressurized gas and used mantles instead of wicks, he bought the patent and improved it. He came out with a portable table lamp version in 1909, and when the car-camping craze took off in the late 1910s and early 1920s, sales soared.

In 1923, Coleman invented the fold-up camp stove, the grandfather of the self-lighting, propane-fueled version of today. The Coleman company actively promoted camping by providing a 64-page "Coleman Motor Camping Manual" by Frank Brimmer.

The manual sold for 25 cents and was filled with advice on what to bring along, how to select a campsite, etc. As time passed, the Coleman company continued to add products to its camping line.

Camping in an Empire 6

Despite hundreds of devices to make it easy, car camping was no picnic. For one thing, the roads into the wilderness were extremely primitive.

When Albert Schuler, the general manager of Santa Barbara's Home Telephone and Telegraph Company, loaded his new Empire 6 roadster with 300 pounds of camping and fishing gear in May 1916 and headed for San Marcos Pass, he had high hopes that the powerful car would conquer

The stylishly-dressed Conover family and friends, circa 1920, find the window of their automobile is a handy place to display their stringer of trout.

A Texas family with their new camper conversion of a Model TT. It had the same engine and transmission as a regular Model T. Note the bedspring frame that secures the children in the back but folds down when the tent is set up. (Library of Congress)

Unfolded, the camp auto provided a kitchen for mom and beds for the family. An electric cord plugged into the automobile powers the light bulb hanging from a branch used as a pole. (Library of Congress)

all obstacles. With him were friend Carl Geiser, *Morning Press* reporter Oscar W. Smith, and Smith's son, Dale. That evening the muscular car negotiated the tortuous San Marcos Road to reach the summit in 42 minutes, a new record. Smith later wrote that he was astonished at the "ease with which the big car rounded the difficult turns and took the steep grades."

The party was headed for a fishing trip on the north side of the San Rafael range beyond Los Olivos. By the time they reached the road up to Zaca Creek, however, it was dark and the road was difficult to find. The fact that a farmer had planted barley over a section of the road didn't help. After several false turns in barley high enough to cover the hood of the car, they found the road again only to become mired in mud caused by a broken irrigation pipe farther up the canyon.

Extricating themselves from the mud, they next had to find the nearly invisible road up the ridge east of Zaca Peak. Smith reported, "In places the road ran alongside the hill at such an angle that it was necessary for the three passengers to lean out on the inside running board to keep it from rolling down the bank."

Eventually they reached a pine forest not far from the summit and pitched camp about three miles from Ranger's Peak in the Santa Barbara National Forest.

The next morning the fishermen continued on foot to Fir Canyon and Davy Brown Creek and caught their limit of rainbow trout. Returning to the mighty Empire 6 at dusk, they loaded up the car and headed back to Santa Barbara, racing a jackrabbit half way down the trail. In his report Smith enthused, "The country is one of the most ideal camping grounds in the southern part of the state .... [and] the Empire 6 was really marvelous."

Over time the 1922 auto camp evolved into Santa Barbara Trailer Park, a residential community for many years. In 2013, a portion of it returned to its roots to become Santa Barbara Auto Camp, which features "glamping" accommodations in luxurious Airstream Trailers. (Courtesy John Woodward)

Auto Transformation

It started out as a trickle and soon became a flood. Automobiles were pouring through Santa Barbara. The local garages kept track of those who stayed to patronize the hotels, but city officials had their eyes on those who passed on by to camp along the roadsides or in farmer's fields far outside of town.

When City Councilman A.W. Dozier returned from an auto tour in 1915, he reported that he had encountered thousands of motor parties and shared camps with hundreds of people from throughout the country. Mindful of the lost business potential of motorists just passing through, Dozier recommended that the city designate a piece of land for an auto camp. Campers who stopped in Santa Barbara for the night would "lay in a supply of groceries, take in our theaters, spend a little money, and get an idea of what Santa Barbara

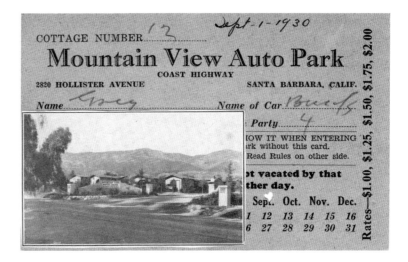

Mountain View Auto Park opened on the west side of Mission Creek in 1925. Today the property is a shopping center once anchored by a grocery store. (Courtesy John Fritsche)

Flapper campers pose beside their car at the Santa Barbara Auto Camp, which opened in 1922 due to the tremendous response to the 1919 City Campground across the street.

really is," he said.

No immediate action was taken on Dozier's idea although a young man named James L. Hawkins opened a camp in connection with his auto supply station at Cacique and Salinas streets. He put in a grocery store and installed water, telephone, gas, light and sewer connections.

In 1919, the city, cognizant that more than 100 motorists a day were bypassing Santa Barbara, finally opened its own camp at Alamar and today's De la Vina streets. (This part of De la Vina was originally named Hollister. State Street did not extend past Constance and the western part of today's State Street was also named Hollister.)

By 1920, the camp included a central lodge with a shady porch furnished with tables and chairs. Inside, campers could use gas plates for cooking, dish towels, dishpans and a large sink. Ironing boards and irons were available, and there were two laundry tubs, a porcelain bathtub, and several showers. Hot water was supplied from a gas water heater.

City Campground also provided the following: for the children, a large sandbox and swings; for the motorist/ mechanic, a pit; for the laundress, facilities for drying clothes; and for the city, potential home buyers. In July 1920, city officials claimed, "Over eighteen thousand dollars worth of real estate has been sold … as a direct result of the Auto Park."

City Campground, located underneath shady oaks on the east bank of Mission Creek, was soon overflowing, so Santa Barbara Auto Camp opened across the street in 1922. In 1925, two more auto camps opened in the immediate area, and businesses catering to autoists proliferated.

Montecito

While Hollister Avenue was the western gateway to Santa Barbara, the eastern gateway lay along the coast highway in Montecito. In 1923, Ida Lietzow capitalized

In addition to Montecito Auto Camp, a gauntlet of advertising sprung up along Coast Highway in Montecito. (Courtesy Santa Barbara Bank and Trust)

By the 1940s, Montecito Trailer Camp dubbed its location "Where the Mountains Meet the Sea." Located at 880 Coast Highway, it featured a fine café and dancing every night. Rates ranged from 25 cents to $1.00 per night. Martin Slaughter was the manager.

on the auto-camp craze that was sweeping the nation and developed Montecito Auto Camp on a strip of land that today houses Olive Mill Plaza. Her small store fronted the coast highway (Coast Village Road) and six wood-floored tents descended toward Spring Street (which once lay south of today's Coast Village Circle.)

In that year, only two gas stations and six houses faced the entire stretch of the coast highway between Olive Mill and Hot Springs roads. In 1929, Martin Bonato joined the tourist camp business with Marty's Auto Court, which stood at today's 1155 Coast Village Road. Businesses catering to autoists soon multiplied and crowded together along the roadway.

American advertisers were quick to capitalize on the new mode of transportation as well. As paved highways began connecting the hubs of civilization, advertisements began appearing on the sides of barns and covered bridges. Billboards blaring their messages in loud colors appeared on land leased from farmers and ranchers, and businesses competed through a plethora of signage.

Not everyone was pleased.

Beautifying the Highway

*E*ver since travel writer Charles Nordhoff (1830-1901) had touted Santa Barbara as a health spa in his 1873 book, *California: For Health, Pleasure, and Residence,* city leaders had seen the wisdom in making and keeping Santa Barbara beautiful. In Montecito, John Alexander Jameson, a transplant from Illinois, took this wisdom to heart. He was instrumental in the formation of the County Planning Commission and in laying the groundwork for the Montecito Association, a civic improvement and preservation organization, as well as the Montecito Water District and subsequent construction of the Doulton Tunnel and Juncal Dam.

By the late 1920s, auto traffic spilling down or chugging up Ortega Hill and along today's Coast Village Road had increased 100-fold. In 1928, the highway through Montecito

In 1928 the Montecito Parkway began at the intersection of Olive Mill Road with the Coast Highway. (Courtesy CalTrans)

consisted of three lanes (the center one for passing), and it still couldn't keep up with the traffic. The state wanted more lanes to accommodate more traffic; however, trucks already roared past roadside businesses imperiling locals and tourists alike.

County Director of Planning, L. Deming Tilton, advanced the concerns of Jameson and many Montecitans

The design of the Montecito Parkway kept local traffic and homes shielded from Highway 101 by landscaping. (Courtesy CalTrans)

The Standard Station on today's Los Patos Way across from the Andrée Clark Bird Refuge won many awards.

when he said that the approaches to the city had become shabbier and shabbier each year. In his report to the County Planning Commission, Tilton wrote, "Montecito rebels at the prospect of this once-delightful, tree-bordered old carriage road becoming a barren, fume-filled canyon of blatant signs, malodorous restaurants, flimsy auto camps and tourist hotels."

The answer, Jameson and the Commission believed, was to create a triple roadway; one for through traffic and two on each side for local businesses. The highway was to become a parkway with planting strips on each side and in the median. The report said that the parkway was to be designed "to insulate private property from the noise, fumes, glare, and hazards of highway traffic" by creating a screen of attractively landscaped vegetation. Both frontage roads were to be bordered with vegetation as well.

The plan was approved December 30, 1930, and Jameson spent the next several years leading the crusade to raise monies and secure the property rights for the project. The first phase, extending from Olive Mill Road to San Ysidro Road, was completed two months after Jameson died in 1937. Plans to extend the parkway to Sheffield Drive were not completed until 1948 and lasted only six years before that section was modified for a freeway that included off-ramps and on-ramps.

Roadside Improvements

Throughout the nation, local organizations worked diligently to improve the roadways. Several groups formed to promote controls on billboard advertising, finding them unattractive and unsafe. Signage was not the only concern, however. The roadsides needed to be beautified through plantings and maintenance. Nationwide, women's organizations and others were called on to organize cleanup campaigns.

In 1930, Bam's Auto Court on Hollister Avenue (today's State Street) boasted 40 cabins on four acres of walnut trees, a grocery, restaurant, and community hall. (Courtesy John Fritsche)

In Santa Barbara, besides a campaign against road signs, the Plans and Planting Branch (P&P) of the Community Arts Association sought to encourage the beautification of roadside businesses as well.

In 1930, civic leader Pearl Chase, chair of the P&P wrote, "The Plans and Planting Branch of the Community Arts Association of Santa Barbara is working in behalf of the ever-increasing numbers who travel the highways for pleasure to improve the character of commercial buildings near towns

In the 1950s, Bam's Court catered to modern trailers and offered a selection of cottages to travelers. (Courtesy John Fritsche)

and on the rural highways. … It is frequently remarked that the highways of California are fast becoming lined with cheap and unsightly commercial establishments … [that] seldom serve their purpose most efficiently and with the least possible offense to the eye."

There was much to offend the eye along Santa Barbara's roads, so the P&P decided to focus on one area, auto camps. Eleven auto camps in Montecito, Goleta, and Santa Barbara were surveyed in 1930, and a statewide architectural competition to create artistically pleasing auto camps was announced. Unfortunately, it was cancelled at the last minute, but the P&P regrouped and shifted its focus to service stations.

Working with multiple organizations throughout the County, the P&P initiated a campaign to promote cleaner and better-landscaped gas stations. A competition offered cash prizes to those who entered. Stations were rated, and the ratings were published. Touting the slogan, "High-quality gas and oil doesn't cost anymore at an attractive station than it does at an unattractive one," the P&P hoped to inspire gas station owners to clean up and the public to patronize those who did.

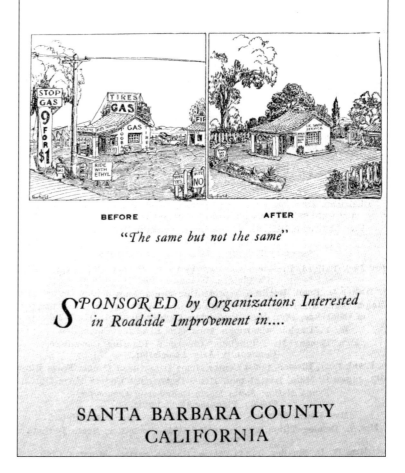

The Plans and Planting Division of the Community Arts Association sponsored a countywide competition to improve the appearance of gas stations.

When the Great Depression descended, California became inundated with a different type of auto camper. Dust Bowl refugees were not touring the state looking at its scenic

The Montecito Parkway plan also eliminated business development from this section of the highway, seen here at the intersection with San Ysidro Road. (Courtesy CalTrans)

wonders. They were hoping for work and sustenance in the agricultural valleys of California and setting up makeshift camps for housing. They were rarely welcomed.

By the time the economic crisis eased in the late 1930s, and travel for pleasure resumed on a larger scale, enthusiasm for auto camps and courts had waned. In 1940, FBI chief J. Edgar Hoover attacked them in an article entitled "Camps of Crime." Many believed that the anonymity of auto court life versus hotel life had led to a class of travelers who were one step above tramps. Communities were no longer so welcoming of these visitors who became known as "tin can tourists."

Auto camps called Hoovervilles sprang up throughout the nation as desperate farm families escaped the Dust Bowl. (Dorothea Lange, Library of Congress)

On June 9, 1909, Alice Huyler Ramsey left the Maxwell Company salesroom on Broadway in New York City in her new Maxwell DA to begin the first transcontinental auto trip piloted exclusively by a woman. (Library of Congress)

Automania: 1909

In the summer of 1909, city promoters were happy to announce, "Santa Barbara is becoming known as an automobile city and all the tourists that pass through here go away singing its praises."

For years the local newspapers had announced the comings and goings of local citizens and visitors via boat and train, as well as the arrivals at the various hotels. Now a new column called "Garage Tips" daily reported such events as "W.L. Graves, a Fresno banker, passed through here yesterday in a Maxwell on his return from Los Angeles." In 1909 Santa Barbara had three garages where touring autoists could reserve space and register their vehicles.

One of these garages, the Higgins Machine Company, was also an agency for new automobiles and announced each delivery as proudly as any new father. July saw Miss

Alice Hart of *El Refugio* in Montecito the happy recipient of a brand new Pope-Hartford 40. By 1909, nearly 300 automobiles were locally owned and more were on the way.

Automobile firsts were filling the record books. On August 7, the first woman to pilot a car across the continent without the aid of a man as driver, Mrs. Alice Huyler Ramsey of Hackensack, New Jersey, and three female friends arrived in San Francisco. Though 59 days had elapsed, the running time was 42 days.

When the now-famous Maxwell DA touring car arrived in Santa Barbara on August 25th, however, it was without Alice, who had hied home to husband and 2-year-old son via train. Mrs. Fred Linz, the wife of the Maxwell-Briscoe Company vice president in San Francisco, had the honor of delivering the car to Los Angeles. Unfortunately, having

One of the first concrete buildings in Santa Barbara, the Mission-style Higgins Machine Company building was a garage, dealership and machine shop at 418 State Street. In these early automobile days, there were no gas stations and autoists had to buy their fuel from the dealer, seen here circa 1905.

Possibly inspired by Alice Ramsey, Betty White, wife of author Stewart Edward White who lived in Santa Barbara, drives her own roadster on the dirt drive leading from their barn-turned-garage off Santa Barbara Street. (Stewart Edward White Collection, SBHM)

The "New Woman" of the late 1890s and early 1900s was not to be denied. Mrs. Arthur Trefisus Ogilvy of Montecito (the former Jessie B. Alexander) was happy to ferry her friends in the new family automobile.

struck some very bad road near Naples, the car was disabled and had to be towed into Santa Barbara, somewhat spoiling the effect of the accomplishment.

At this time, rules regarding automobiles were in their infancy, and drivers' licenses and safety precautions were unknown as the following story illustrates. Blissfully smoking a cigar, R.M. Watkins of Pasadena was driving over the tortuous Casitas Pass in his Buick when a passing youth frantically flagged him down.

Watkins' back seat was on fire! Cigar ash had ignited some waste in the back seat, under which were two five-gallon cans, one filled with gasoline and the other with oil. Grabbing a

canteen of water, Watkins quickly extinguished the flame, thereby avoiding self-immolation and learning the hard way that smoking a cigar in an open car was not terrifically intelligent.

Speed Maniacs

The 1901 advent of the automobile in Santa Barbara had stirred the racing urges of its owners. By July 1909, concerned city officials passed a speed ordinance of 15 mph in the city and 20 mph on the Boulevard (Cabrillo). Trouble was, there were no signs indicating such restrictions until August, when 14 signs were finally installed at various points along roads leading into the city.

Meanwhile the local members of the Automobile Club of America were recruited as deputies by Sheriff Nat Stewart to

Unknown woman on Santa Barbara's Riviera prepares to drive her two black spaniels in an early automobile circa 1903. The steering tiller she is using was quickly becoming extinct and by 1909 had been replaced by the steering wheel.

When the law cracked down on spontaneous street races, enthusiasts organized sanctioned race events like the 1914 Fourth of July race in Lompoc. Arlo Atchison of Santa Barbara converted a 1910 Buick Redbird into this race car and won 3rd place. (Atchison Family Photo Album, SBHM)

help, as the *Morning Press* reported, "put a stop to the reckless driving of machines through the city streets and over the country roads." Stewart wanted to keep the names of these Auto Club deputies secret so speeders would be ignorant of their identities and unable to avoid arrest.

Apparently, inviting members of the Auto Club to control speedsters was like inviting the fox to guard the hen house. At their September 2, 1902 meeting, Auto Club member M.E. Rodehaver railed against his compatriots for breaking the speed ordinance. He said, "We members of the automobile club come up here at every meeting and denounce the speeders as maniacs, murderers and men who should be jailed and then go out on the street and break the city speed ordinance!"

In full dudgeon, Rodehaver continued, "I try to keep within the speed limit and first some little machine whizzes by then another and then some little one-cylinder 'Olds' shows you her heels and you eat the dust of the whole bunch. . . . It is pretty hard for a man driving a high power car to let some little 'one lung' machine pass him even if he is trying to keep from breaking the law. When a man has to eat the dust of every little car in town his good intentions are put to a hard test!"

Some men railed against the speed laws themselves. When William R. Ruess, known to the Southen California racing world as "Wild Bill," was arrested on East Cabrillo Boulevard for speeding in his big Pope-Hartford racer, he denied he was speeding and said the officers had exceeded their authority in arresting him. Having received complaints the previous day about Wild Bill's delusion that East Boulevard was a racetrack, two members of the police force had hidden themselves in a barn at the foot of Anacapa Street where they lay in wait for the appearance of the big car, thereby establishing Santa Barbara's first speed trap.

Arlo Atchison speeds along a dirt street. Arriving in Santa Barbara circa 1912, he and his older brother opened an auto-repair business in 1915. In later years, Arlo's passion for the automobiles of his youth led him to open the Horseless Carriage Restoration Shop in Santa Barbara. (Atchison Family Photo Album, SBHM)

Ruess was arrested for driving an outrageous 30 mph and taken to the police station where he was bailed out by L. Higgins, the local agent for automaker Pope-Hartford.

There was a reason so many citizens of Santa Barbara were apoplectic about speeding autos. Nearly every day during the summer of 1909, the papers reported accidents. Headlines screamed, "CLOSE CALL FOR AUTOISTS AT CASITAS: Speed Maniac Crowds Machine to Edge of Steep Embankment," or "CHINESE CRUSHED TO DEATH BY WHEELS OF AUTOMOBILE: Victim Run Down Yesterday While Alighting From Car on State Street." In September, a Boston bull pup owned by James F. Cornwall, secretary of the Board of Public Works, was crushed under the wheels of a large touring car on East Boulevard. The driver never stopped; instead, he sped away leaving a cloud of dust in place of apologies.

On the Lighter Side

One man was not about to become the victim of a hit and run. When a car belonging to Mrs. Arthur Barlow, a prominent Los Angeles society matron staying at the Potter Hotel, struck the milk wagon of William Müller, it toppled the wagon, shattering the milk bottles and causing Müller's horse to flee in wild-eyed panic. Müller leapt into the unoccupied seat next to the driver of the car and demanded recompense. A German, Müller's command of English was less than perfect, and assurances that he would be paid for his loss went uncomprehended. He insisted he be paid on the spot. The aggravated milkman stubbornly kept his seat until a passing deliveryman for the Hunt Mercantile Company convinced him to accept a promissory note from Mrs. Barlow.

Müller had second thoughts, however, after he retrieved his frightened horse and surveyed the damage to his wagon whose wheels now wobbled and front axle was badly bent.

Early automobiles, like this one, strongly resembled horse drawn carriages.

Mission Transfer ferried passengers on excursions through the new Hope Ranch subdivision and Potter Golf Club. The advent of the car in Santa Barbara changed the ways people did business.

Narrow, winding Eucalyptus Hill was closed to motor traffic by city ordinance, but that didn't stop some Montecito autoists from taking the shortcut to town.

Determined, Müller turned his damaged rig and headed for the Boulevard. The *Morning Press* reported, "Driving up to the main entrance of the Potter where a great number of the guests were seated on the veranda, he left his horse and battered milk wagon and with his face covered with blood, he went inside looking for Mrs. Barlow. He evidently found her for he came out in a few minutes, a broad smile of satisfaction spreading over his blood-smeared countenance."

On the issue of auto rules, Montecitan turned against fellow Montecitan when Francis Eaton (son of artist Charles Frederick Eaton) turned in Huron Rock, owner of the local Cadillac agency, for driving over Eucalyptus Hill, which had been closed to auto traffic by a city ordinance. Rock was fined only $10 as this was the first arrest for that offense.

The Auto Club (in spite of the lead feet of some of its members) supported auto activities, safety rules, and participation in public-spirited events. The club arranged for a series of auto races to be held on the Boulevard to promote tourism. Francis T. Underhill of Montecito, who had served on the commission that had drafted the traffic rules and regulations for the city of New York, lobbied for similar rules for Santa Barbara.

On August 19, 1909, members volunteered their time and vehicles for an excursion for the children of St. Vincent's Orphanage. The *Morning Press* reported that flags adorned each of the 25 cars, which ran up and down the Boulevard to Booth's Point, "the children tingling with delight."

Probably the most unusual incident involving auto enthusiasts also occurred in August. A large touring car from Los Angeles drove up to the First Christian Church and presented Pastor Sumner T. Martin with a most unusual request. Mr. Ernest Davidson Henderson and Miss Charlotte Carrie Mills desired that the preacher marry them as they sat in the machine. The *Morning Press* reported, "Rev. Martin, being of an obliging disposition, did as they wished, and they drove off rejoicing." Now that's automania!

Despite the completion of the Rincon Causeway in 1912, some autoists continued to drive on the sands. When the tides came in, old fashioned horsepower came to the rescue. (Atchison Family photo album, SBHM)

For such a small town, Santa Barbara, seen here from the Mesa in 1902, has had more than its share of influential citizens.
(Library of Congress)

They Made a Difference

From its inception, Santa Barbara has been blessed with a pantheon of civic and community benefactors and prominent artists and artisans who have ensured its well-being, preserved its heritage, and influenced its development. During Spanish days, the generosity and patronage of José de la Guerra y Noriega, commander of the Presidio, supported the people of the pueblo. Newcomers during the early American days, such as Colonel William Welles Hollister, Mary Ashley, John P. Stearns and José Lobero, were promoters of business, beneficence and culture. They, and others like them, transformed the pueblo into a bustling town. In the 1910s and '20s, a new group of magnanimous philanthropists, cultural leaders, and city designers developed the town into one of the most highly regarded cities of California.

Following are the stories behind five incredible, but lesser-known, lights who made a difference to the community of their day. The exceptional Dr. Jane Edna Spaulding, who described herself as having "inherited a reasonable amount of poverty" gave unstintingly to others and ensured the early success of Cottage Hospital. The well-to-do Park family attempted to preserve a culture and provide for a variety of community needs. Albert and Adele Herter established and enriched Santa Barbara's artistic and cultural traditions, while Alexander Harmer preserved Santa Barbara's Spanish heritage through his gifted brushwork and created the underpinnings for Santa Barbara's growing artist colony. Roland Sauter's vision and talent helped enrich and shape the architectural landscape of the city.

The influence of these men and women is discernable in the durability and outgrowth of the works they left behind.

In 1892, Dr. Jane Edna Spaulding, standing on lower steps, took charge of the new Cottage Hospital, which had opened the previous December.

(Santa Barbara Historical Museum)

The Unexpected Dr. Jane Edna Spaulding

On a perfect Santa Barbara day in September 1913, Captain Colís Vazquez of the *Otter* cast off from Stearns Wharf carrying a hermetically sealed copper urn containing the ashes of Dr. Jane Edna Spaulding, the much-loved first superintendent of Santa Barbara Cottage Hospital. As she wished, a small party of intimate friends consigned her mortal remains to the waters of the Santa Barbara Channel.

Upon her death a month earlier, a friend had written, "She was a rare woman, strong in her convictions of duty, capable beyond most women, tender and loyal as a child in her affections; always ready to help anyone in distress, never saving herself if she could in anyway add to the comfort or happiness of another."

Jane Spaulding's contributions to the community were made quietly and without fanfare. Her actions rarely showed up in the newspapers and her activities did not make the society pages. Consequently, 100 years later, little about her life and work is generally known. A deeper look into her past, however, reveals a brilliant and witty woman who found the courage to break the strictures of respectability to find her true place in the world.

Jane Edna Spaulding was 60 years old when she returned to Santa Barbara to become Cottage Hospital's first supervisor.

The Respectable Jane Spaulding

Jane Spaulding was born in January 1832 to Stern and Caroline (Dewey) Spaulding in Lewiston, New York, the birthplace of Niagara Falls and the final stop on the Underground Railroad. By 1850, her family had five children and owned an 80-acre farm. She was born at a time of great change in the United States. The Industrial Revolution was gaining steam, and the Age of Reform tackled issues ranging from temperance to women's rights to abolition. As the American frontier continued to expand westward, the

When Dr. Richard Hall (marked by an x) finally agreed to open a surgery at Cottage Hospital in 1895, he contributed to the financial success and security of the fledgling institution.

Spaulding family was drawn to new opportunities and moved to Michigan.

By 1860, Jane's parents were raising sheep for wool and growing wheat, rye, oats and Indian corn in Adams, Michigan, while she was living with her uncle Volney who was farming in Palmyra. Stern eventually gave up on farming and moved to Palmyra to run a hotel and sell liquor. Jane, meanwhile, recognized that she had to earn a living.

In an 1866 interview, she stated, "I inherited a reasonable amount of poverty, an inheritance that I have always retained and still possess and which was a constant stimulus to all my efforts. Necessity, therefore, being a continual reminder that something must be done whereby I might earn my bread and butter, I naturally looked around as boys do, endeavoring to find something for which I had some attraction and adaptation.

"You will probably say that I looked around very much as girls do, when I tell you that the first object to which I was attracted was a young man. The attraction not proving mutual, something else must be thought of and it was at this time that the idea of studying medicine first occurred to me."

When Jane made known her desire to family and friends, her father worried that the work would be too difficult and her friends were aghast! Would she really compromise her respectability in such a way?

"Consequently," she said, "the idea was for a time relinquished, and I became a respectable school-mum in a stable village school, where I remained for four or five years. During those years I grew wiser, whether my pupils did or not, and concluded that respectability was an elephant I could no longer afford to carry."

Jane left the school to become a clerk in a store and was determined to begin studying medicine. The law at the time required that a medical student had to study medicine with a regularly qualified physician for three years and attend two full courses (years) of medical lectures before he or she could receive a degree. She found a physician who was willing to take her on, and he gave her free use of his medical library. She was especially impressed with his fine manikin and skeleton. Studying a minimum of two hours a day and continuing to work a full shift at the store, she was surprised at how much she had learned in a year.

Elizabeth Cady Stanton and Lucretia Mott had organized the first women's rights convention at Seneca Falls in 1848, and women had made various advances in the years following, but little progress had been made regarding the inequality of pay for equal work. Jane said, "I worked [at the store] as many hours a day and did my work equally well as any clerk, and yet received less than half [the pay] of some of the male clerks. … I had frequent controversies with the proprietors during the two years I was in their employ, trying to convince them that I ought to receive as much as a man but they couldn't 'see it and never did.'

"When I left them, they (very generously as they thought) tendered me a present of $50. I replied that I would accept it not as a gift but as a portion of my wages they had hitherto refused to pay."

Our Dear Friend, the Doctor

On November 1, 1863, the New York Medical College for Women opened its doors thanks to founder Dr. Clemence Sophia Lozier, and in March 1865, Jane Edna Spaulding of Coldwater, Michigan, received a degree declaring her a homeopathic physician and surgeon. Homeopathy was a popular and increasingly respected form of medical practice

NEW YORK CITY.—MEDICAL COLLEGE FOR WOMEN, EAST TWELFTH STREET AND SECOND AVENUE—THE ANATOMICAL LECTURE-ROOM.—SEE PAGE 71.

Jane Spaulding listened and took notes on anatomy at the New York Medical College for Women five years before the women pictured in this illustration.
(Library of Congress)

at the time, mainly because the standard practice of the day often relied on ineffective, dangerous, and at times, harmful treatments. Patients of homeopaths generally had much better outcomes.

The commencement exercises were held at New York's Athenaeumn, and the building was crowded, *The New York Times* said, "with an intellectual audience." Commencement speaker Professor Carroll Dunham bid farewell to the class of 15 students and welcomed them as fellow practitioners. He reminded the all-female class that having asserted they were fit to practice medicine, a college was created for them, and now the public would expect them to justify that assertion. "Nothing will secure the public esteem as surely as earnestness and single-minded devotion to the profession," he said. Jane Edna Spaulding took these words to heart.

That same year, Dr. Spaulding secured her first position as a doctor on Lake Erie's Kelleys Island in Ohio. It's economy,

Captain William S. Webb and family took Jane Spaulding under their wing when she became the Kelleys Island doctor. She moved with them to Santa Barbara and then to Larned, Kansas. (Courtesy of Leslie Korenko)

The dock at Kelleys Island, circa 1865 (Courtesy of Leslie Korenko)

established by Datus and Ira Kelley in the 1830s, was based on viniculture, winemaking, quarrying and commercial fishing. Initially, Jane lived and kept her office at the home of Captain William Samuel Webb, a Civil War veteran who had married into the Kelley family. Webb had accumulated quite an income through merchandising and steamboating.

The long road to an M.D. hadn't taken the edge off of Jane's pixie-like sense of humor. One of her business cards in the local newspaper stated, "Miss Spaulding, homeopathic physician, cures all infirmities that flesh is heir to, except chronic laziness. Charges depending on how much she thinks she can get. She guarantees the cure will not be worse than the disease."

From 1865 until 1873, Dr. Spaulding contented herself with caring for the islanders. A February 1867 news account reported that when George Elfers fell off some scaffolding, he was raced to "the office of Miss J.E. Spaulding, who skillfully set the dislocated joint and bound up his other bruises without pain to the patient by successfully administering to him chloroform." In January 1872, she was dealing with an epidemic of mumps.

Then, on September 27, 1873, a news item in the *Islander* announced, "Four of our esteemed fellow citizens, Mr. and Mrs. Webb, son, and the doctor, expect to start for California next Tuesday. They go for health and pleasure, and if they like the climate, country and people, may conclude to remain there. We shall miss them socially very much, and hope they may conclude to return. The doctor, Miss Spaulding, we shall scarcely know how to get along without. We shall not be likely to get another physician that will for a long time earn

Dr. Jane Spaulding poses with the nursing staff on the porch of Cottage Hospital.

announced, "The office of Jane E. Spaulding, M.D. has been removed from Stanley's building to a residence on De la Vina street one door from the corner of Ortega. In this connection we may say that Miss Spaulding has grown in favor as a homeopathic physician since her advent here, and everywhere we hear her spoken of as a lady of marked ability in her profession."

In July 1874, the *Daily Press* reported, "A boy of about 15 years of age who works for Colonel Bond in the Montecito Valley had his arm broken a few days since by a fall from a colt which he had been riding. Jane E. Spaulding, M.D., set the injured limb, and Colonel Bond and family are enthusiastic in the praise of the skillful manner in which it was set."

That same year the California State legislature passed a local option law, which left it up to each community to decide whether to license saloons or not. Dr. Spaulding climbed on the bandwagon promoting an end to saloons in Santa Barbara. After mass meetings and much singing

the confidence of the community that she has in the seven years she has been with us. She will make herself popular in any country, and for this reason we shall not expect her to return."

A Visit to The Promised Land

The Webb family and Dr. Spaulding arrived in Santa Barbara on October 10, 1873 and registered at the one-year-old Occidental Hotel, the largest in the city. Later Jane and the Webbs stayed with relatives of Captain Webb on the outskirts of town, and she quickly acquired three patients. Due to the remote location, she hoped to acquire a horse so she could hang her shingle in town.

The Webbs eventually purchased a home on De la Vina Street, and the June 1874 edition of the *Santa Barbara Press*

Jane and the Webbs stayed at the new Occidental Hotel when they first arrived in Santa Barbara.

Spaulding and the Webbs left Santa Barbara just as transportation was improved by a mule-powered street railway that ran up State Street between Sterns Wharf and Sola Street.

of hymns, she and two other leaders in the cause presented a petition containing the names of the requisite number of legal voters, and the question was placed on the ballot. (Santa Barbarans voted to go dry and then largely ignored the new law, which was later declared unconstitutional.)

Jane wrote enthusiastic letters about Santa Barbara to her friends at Kelleys Island. "The longer I remain, the better I like it," she wrote. "Mrs. Webb says I like even the dust and fogs and won't admit the fleas are not the most agreeable company…. Well, what is the use, I came here to live and I am not going to live in a place I don't like.

"Now about this promised land," she continued, "nothing, it seems to me, can be more enjoyable than this climate. True, it is a little monotonous, but then we can stand the monotony of pleasant days with better grace than that of cold, stormy ones." She reported that it only rained at night, and, anticipating Lerner and Loewe by 80 years, said "by nine the morning fog has disappeared." In short, there was simply not a more congenial spot….

The Webbs, missing their adult children, decided to leave in spring of 1875. The previous December, Jane had contracted a painful eye ailment, which she believed was the consequence of a severe cold. She was confined to a darkened

When Dr. Spaulding set up her offices in the Stanley Building in the 1870s, Santa Barbara still resembled a Wild West town of dirt streets, wooden sidewalks, and false-fronted buildings.

room for three months, so painful was exposure to light, and it was feared she would lose the use of both eyes. One eye was completely restored but the other eye only partially. One source (unconfirmed) says that in her later years she lost the eye altogether and had a glass eye. Though her eyes were much better by spring, Jane, too, returned to Kelleys Island.

Larned, Kansas Interlude

In August 1879, Dr. Spaulding returned to Santa Barbara for a very short time. She opened an office in the Pierce block (600 block) of State Street and resided at the Arlington Hotel. By 1880 she was living with her brother Truman's family in Gibson, Illinois. In 1881, the Webb family moved to Larned, Kansas, to be closer to their married daughter, Sara Rush, and her family, and by 1884 Jane had joined them.

Built on the route of the Atchison, Topeka and Santa Fe Railroad in 1873, Larned was a bustling center of commerce and boasted 50 businesses by the mid-1880s. Captain William Webb was twice elected mayor of Larned and served as councilman for many years. Jane went into business with Dr. J. M. Cummins and had her office at his home, site of today's Jordaan Memorial (once Cummins) Library.

Jane maintained correspondence with her friends on Kelleys Island, and the 1885 *Islander* reported, "The many friends of Miss J.E. Spaulding (who was our practicing physician a few years since) will be pleased to learn that she is half owner and proprietor of a drug store in Larned, Kansas. She reports business good and that Larned has doubled in population in the past year."

Jane returned to a Santa Barbara that was busy growing into a modern town. Brick buildings lined State Street, and electric trams had replaced the mule-drawn railway.

The 1890 Trades Fair was one of many community fund-raisers for construction of Cottage Hospital.

In 1892, Jane received a letter from Mary Ashley, one of the founders and president of the board of directors of the new Cottage Hospital, which had opened for business in Santa Barbara on December 8, 1891. The board, which had tried to supervise the running of the hospital, realized they needed an on-call physician and professional to act as superintendent. Mary offered Dr. Spaulding the princely sum of $75 a month plus room and board at the hospital if she would take the position. Jane, now in her 60th year, accepted.

Return to Camelot

Jane arrived in the fall of 1892 and set to work. Cottage Hospital was not on a solid financial footing, and the general economy was experiencing a depression as a consequence of the collapse of the 1887 land boom. The hospital relied on annual donation day in December and financial support for free beds by several organizations in town. The woman who had demanded equal pay for equal work voluntarily reduced her salary to reduce the debt. Also looming on the horizon were reports that Dr. Richard Hall was planning to open his own private hospital, which would create competition for Cottage Hospital.

In her annual report for the year ending in 1894, Dr. Spaulding reported that the hospital had served 157 patients of which 10 died. Proving that age hadn't dulled her wit, she stated wryly, "Of the deaths, all were in the last stages of disease when admitted. While the records of the Hospital would make a better showing if such cases were not received, the purposes for which it was established would not be carried out were they refused admission."

That year, in addition to donations of money, the hospital received gifts ranging from newspapers donated by Dr. Southwick to three pairs of bedroom slippers given by the Faulkner sisters. A list of miscellaneous donations showed

As Santa Barbara continued to grow, Cottage Hospital found itself adding space by enclosing porches. Jane, in dark dress, poses with her staff of nurses.

that Mrs. M. Waters gave one gallon of mixed pickles, Brooks and Morton grocery sent a sack of potatoes, and Mrs. Woodbridge delivered a basket of apples. Mrs. Charles C. (Helen) Park, of a more practical nature, generously donated two chiffoniers, two oil stoves, three tin washbasins, three cuspidors, and one hot water bag. Sandwiched between Miss Bigelow's donation of two glasses of jelly and Mrs. George Russell's flower vase was one-quarter block of land adjoining hospital grounds and valued at $1,200, given by Mr. and Mrs. Hugh D. Vail.

Nevertheless, in December the *Morning Press* published Mary Ashley's announcement that despite the most economical of plans, under the "judicious management of Dr. J.E. Spalding [sic] and the board of lady directors, … it

miss McGregor

Dr. Spalding

Dr. Spaulding and
her staff pose on the
porch of the hospital.

has been impossible to make ends meet. We now appeal to the citizens and friends of this good work to contribute to the liquidation of this debt."

Then in 1895, Dr. Richard Hall, having rethought plans to establish his own hospital, set up a surgery at Cottage Hospital. His presence increased business and income. Dr. Spaulding reported, "The Hospital was never in a more prosperous condition than at present. For the first time in its history, the balance at the close of the year is on the credit side of the ledger. Still, the surplus is not so large as to tempt the

Treasurer to abscond, or the Superintendent to embezzle."

In 1896, business was on a solid footing until Dr. Hall suddenly died, and the hospital was forced to take austerity measures for 1897. According to historian Walker Tompkins, Dr. Spaulding took no salary that year, and the nursing program was suspended. Jane reported that no patients were admitted who didn't pay in advance or had a responsible person vouch for them. "Doctors have been known to pay office rent and support families on air," she wrote, "but hospitals are not maintained in that ethereal manner.

An unknown couple stands in front of construction of the second Cottage Hospital.

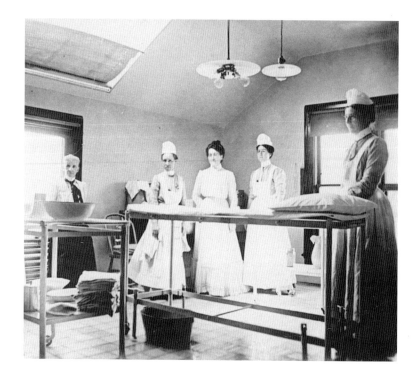

Dr. Spaulding and her staff inspect a surgery at Cottage Hospital.

Promises to pay do not settle grocer's bills." The surplus in the treasury for 1897 was 51 cents.

The statewide depression had eased significantly by 1898, and the hospital was on its way to becoming self-sustaining. By 1909, it was clear that a larger, more modern version of the hospital was needed. Mrs. Helen Kittridge Park gave voice to the idea and a capital campaign was initiated. Jane was an ardent supporter of the new hospital and wished for nothing more than to see it completed.

In 1911, Jane retired due to increasingly debilitating effects of arteriosclerosis, though she continued to live at the hospital. On July 31, 1913, the new hospital, touted by the *Morning Press* as being "of imposing proportions and pleasing design," hosted a formal opening. Jane was the guest of honor at the opening's tea reception and the first patient admitted to the new hospital.

Twenty-one days later, Dr. Jane Edna Spaulding died. The

When the new Cottage Hospital was completed, the old building, seen here in the background, became a home for nurses.

annual report for that year says of her, "By many and varied services she manifested her attachment to the hospital and her belief in its behalf. She was a woman of strict honor and integrity, and united to an iron perseverance that overcame all discouragements [was] a tenderness of heart that showed itself to those who came in close contact with her."

Jane's early friends feared she would lose her respectability by becoming a doctor, but she found the courage to throw off that yoke. "When we wish to do a thing," she once wrote, "instead of asking our neighbors if it is respectable, let us first ask ourselves if it is right. For if it be right, we can very easily make it respectable." The amazing Jane Edna Spaulding embodied the very essence of respectability.

Dr. Charles Caldwell Park and Helen Kittridge Park (Courtesy of Eleanor Park Beronius)

The Parks of Park Lane

Park Lane in Montecito is named for the Park family and retains its allée of eucalyptus trees.

The *Morning Press* of September 14, 1917, reported, "Santa Barbara residents whose interests are so wide and their friends so numerous that their absence will be regretted by many are Mr. and Mrs. C.C. Park and family who are leaving for the East with prospects of long residence there." Indeed, the Park family, who had moved to Santa Barbara in 1893, had already left an indelible mark on Santa Barbara at that time, and, luckily, 1917 was not their final departure.

Charles Caldwell Park was born in Allegheny City, Pennsylvania, in 1860. His father, James Park Jr., was one of two brothers whose business ventures focused on the importation, sale, and manufacture of various metals.

While most of Charles Caldwell Park's brothers entered the family business, Charles graduated from Cornell University in 1883 and went on to study medicine at New York's Bellevue Hospital. He completed his medical training abroad, studying at universities in Vienna, Austria, and Heidelberg, Germany. In 1886, he married Helen Kittridge of Massachusetts (Cornell Class of 1886), and soon the couple moved to New York, where Charles began to practice medicine.

In Santa Barbara

In 1893, the Park family pulled up stakes and moved to Santa Barbara where Dr. Park set up a medical practice. They rented in town for three years before buying 27 acres northwest of what became Park Lane. To design their home, they hired fledgling architect Francis Wilson, who later became quite renowned for his architectural work designing several Harvey Houses and other buildings for the Santa Fe Railroad.

For the Parks, Wilson created a one-story house built entirely of redwood. The house included a library and a wing of bedrooms for the children, who would eventually number seven. The property also included detached servants' quarters, a small dairy, a gardener's cottage, and a reservoir. A lemon orchard stood on most of the remaining acreage. They named their new estate after a German resort town on the Rhine, *Karlsruhe,* which translates as "Charles' Rest."

Later, Wilson would design a memorial to the Parks' deceased sons, Roy Harrison Park and Charles Caldwell Park Jr. who had died in infancy. Though simplified from Wilson's original intent, the Beaux Arts fountain was placed on the main highway into Montecito because Park wanted to provide refreshment for man and beast. Many a horse and rider benefited from the fountain before changes to the roadway

The Parks' daughter Elizabeth was a director of the new and improved Montecito Home Club that stood on the southwest corner of San Ysidro and East Valley roads. (Montecito Association History Committee)

Francis Wilson designed the house at Karlsruhe, the Park family estate

Friday night teen dances were popular events throughout the years of the Montecito Home Club. Seen here, left to right, Joyce Polloreña, Carol Polloreña dancing with Dennis Ensign, and Jean Polloreña dancing with her brother Bob as Michael Buggy taps in. (Courtesy of Maureen Masson)

A descendent of Presidio soldiers, Felipa Polloreña taught at the first Montecito Home Club and worked to preserve the old Spanish culture of her forebears. (Montecito Association History Committee)

destroyed the pipes. Today that location is the corner of Cabrillo Boulevard and Channel Drive.

Charles established a relationship with Dr. Richard Hall of the newly completed Cottage Hospital, and Helen Park joined the St. Cecilia Club, which raised funds to furnish a free bed at the hospital for those without means. She became the club's president in 1917, and Dr. Park gave medical aid to families who couldn't afford care. He became known for charitable work done quietly and without fanfare.

Park also invested in business property on State Street and ranch land in Carpinteria and Santa Ynez. The Parks soon became an integral part of social, cultural and philanthropic life in Santa Barbara and Montecito.

In 1908, Helen Park became president of an effort to create a community center called the Montecito Community Home Club, whose clubhouse was renovated from an old store building on East Valley Road across the street from today's Montecito Hall. It offered a reading and game room as well as a reception room with a piano. Classes for children included cooking lessons by Felipa Romero Polloreña as well as sewing classes. Felipa also worked to preserve Spanish culture and had introduced the old Spanish dances and costumes at a fundraiser for the St. Cecilia Club given at Montecito Hall four years earlier.

The Home Club proved extremely popular, and it soon became apparent that a larger facility was needed. In 1914, Mrs. James Hobert (Laura) Moore (later Knight) paid for the construction of a Craftsman-style clubhouse on the southwest corner of East Valley and San Ysidro roads. The Parks' daughter Elizabeth became one the directors.

Preserving Spanish Culture

As the Parks became increasingly involved in the community, they became fascinated by Santa Barbara's Spanish history. Charles learned Spanish and enjoyed speaking with the old Spanish residents of Montecito. They both worked to preserve the older culture, and to that end, in July 1907, Mrs. Park hosted a dance for 12 couples at the Santa Barbara Country Club (then on Channel Drive). In addition to the standard waltzes and two-steps, the event included instruction for the steps of La Jota, a lively folk dance from the Aragon province in Spain.

In 1914, Dr. Park began hosting Christmas parties for the descendents of *Californio* families, mostly elderly ladies. In 1922, the year of the eighth party, a plethora of historic names–from Arrellanes to Valenzuela–enjoyed a feast of

Dr. Park sits front and center with his guests, descendents of the Old Spanish families in Santa Barbara and Montecito.

Christmas luncheon at the Park house was always a festive affair.

turkey and all its "fixin's" topped off by dessert of mince pie *en el modo de la fiesta de Dr. Park.*

Tables were cheerfully decorated and all the guests received Christmas favors. After dinner the floor was cleared for dancing, and the lilting strains of "Sobre las Olas" (Over the Waves) enticed the guests to respond to the rhythm of the waltz. The old songs were sung, the old dances danced and the old days brought to life.

Then Dr. Park was presented with a surprise, a special rendition of *Los Pastores*, staged by his guests as a way of saying thanks. Performed in the traditional way and using the old words and music, it featured Juan Calderon as El Bartolo and Francisco Lopez in the dramatic role of Lucifero.

In her column in the *Morning Press*, Julia Redington wrote, "The little group of players managed to give the real feeling of the Christmas mystery, and from the moment when they marched in singing "Adeste Fideles" to the last tableau in which they crooned a lullaby to the Holy Child ('El Nino Jesús'), they played their parts with real skill."

Legends from the Past

Stirred by the stories he heard from his Spanish guests, Dr. Park was inspired to write two books detailing the history and legends of Spanish California. Using the pseudonym Carl Gray, he wrote *A Plaything of the Gods (1912),* which tells the story of one of California's most notorious bandits, Joaquin Murieta.

Almost all "Old-Timers" in California had a (tall) tale or two to tell of their encounter with the dashing Murieta who had visited every town, stayed in every hotel, drunk in every bar, and had a hideout in every county.

In Santa Barbara, legend says Murieta had a secret lair up the coast at the old Ortega Adobe at Arroyo Hondo. For entertainment he'd ride into Spanish Town in Montecito to attend fandangos underneath the *parra grande* (big grapevine) at the Dominguez abode. One night, as he was gamboling to "La Jota" with a beautiful señorita, word reached him that the sheriff was coming to arrest him. Acting quickly, he broke a twig off the grapevine to use as a whip, vaulted onto his horse and sped away up one of the canyons. Riding all night, he made his way to a hidden camp at the base of Big Pine Mountain. There he stuck the grapevine whip in the ground and it took root. Supposedly, it is still growing in Grapevine Canyon.

A review in *The New York Times* of *A Plaything of the Gods* reported, "Mr. Gray has endeavored, he says, to paint a true…. picture of Joaquin's life. He exhibits the man as

Alexander Harmer painted a the pivotal scene in the book in which three vicious placer miners sneak up on Carmela and Joaquin.

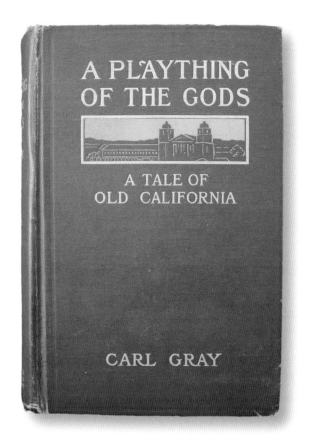

Park used the pseudonym Carl Gray to write his tale of Joaquin Murieta.

one who, naturally kind and gentle, was so changed by the persecution and brutality he suffered that he became almost fiendish in his cruelty."

Alexander Harmer illustrated Dr. Park's book. Harmer had married into one of the old *Californio* families and his work from that time forward chronicled the life and culture of Santa Barbara's original European settlers. His drawings and paintings appeared in many publications of the day.

Budding Playwright

In 1915 Dr. Park wrote a second book, *Tales of Old California,* a series of short stories set in Santa Barbara. In 1917, he developed one of these stories, "Doña Perritos, the Dog Woman," into a play and presented it at the two-year-old Country Playhouse in Montecito. Called *Atonement,*

Thanks to Mrs. William M. (Eleanor) Graham of the original Bellosguardo estate, the Country Playhouse was built in 1914 near Middle Road in Montecito. Designed in part by Francis Wilson and featuring three murals by Albert Herter, it was a popular venue until it burned down a scant 4 years later.

it featured local talent in the dramatic roles and included dancing and singing.

Dr. Park was much influenced by popular literary, stage and film styles of the times and *Atonement* had all the features of a musical melodrama. The *Morning Press* summarized the plot as follows: "The play is written around the tragic story of Felisa Escharren. The plot develops from the incident of Felisa's borrowing, in a fit of girlish vanity, a pearl necklace which is the only thing of value remaining in her family, after the wild extravagance of her father, now dead, had dissipated their fortune."

Tragedy followed when the pearls were stolen by an unscrupulous party guest. In regaining them, Felisa kills the thief and goes quite mad with remorse. She is driven from her home and wanders the hills with only a pack of dogs for companionship.

Country Playhouse

Dr. C. C. Park's Play,

"The Atonement"

Saturday, February 17th, at 8:30

Tickets on Sale at Box Office Country Playhouse, Feb. 14, 15, 16, 17, from 11 to 2 o'Clock

Gift Shop Seat Sale
Wednesday to Saturday, Inclusive
Admission $3.00

Alexander Harmer painted a scene for Park's "Doña Perritos, the Dog Woman," the story that became the play Atonement. (gift of Carl Gray Park, SBHM)

Fiesta Special

In 1928, Dr. Park's adaptation of *A Plaything of the Gods* was staged by the Drama Branch of the Community Arts Association. It was called "Joaquin Murieta" and played all five days of Fiesta to rave reviews.

In an interview for the *Morning Press*, Dr. Park said, "I think that people should know something about Murieta. He is one of the great figures of Old California history." Dr. Park admitted that since he wrote his book, he had heard many conflicting stories regarding Murieta's life, but he believed his to be the most authentic.

He also said, "I think that it is a fine thing that we can

"JOAQUIN MURIETA"

Presented by

Drama Branch, Community Arts Association

LOBERO THEATRE

Old Spanish Days

Santa Barbara, California   July 31, August 1, 2, 3, and 4.

1928

Fifteen years later, the great earthquake of 1812 destroys the mission, and Felisa is so shocked that her reason returns. She remembers where the pearls are hidden and gives them to the padre, to be used in the restoration of the mission. Her atonement complete, she falls back and dies.

Heady stuff, indeed, … and all accompanied by singing and dancing and a climactic performance of the Contradanza. Best of all, the cast was composed of such luminous local talents as Ester and Gardiner Hammond, Miss Delfina de la Guerra Dibblee, and Mr. Joel Fithian, who played the amatory ranchman.

Dr. Park's play was the high point of the season and numerous dinner parties were given at the hotels, country clubs, and private estates before hosts and guests flocked to the Country Playhouse for the much-anticipated performance.

At teas like these at Tipperary, Charles Caldwell Park learned the tales of Old California, which he tried to preserve through his books and plays.

give the play here using the Old Californians in the cast. It will assure us of the real songs and dances of the native people."

Charles Meredith, a well-known leading man of the time, came to direct and took on the role of Joaquin Murieta. The cast numbered 140, and between the singing, dancing, costumes, and set, the entire production approached extravaganza status.

The reviews were glowing: "From the moment the curtain went up until it fell down on the last scene, 'Joaquin Murieta,' Santa Barbara's own play, ... held the audience in a grip that at times was too tense to be comfortable.

"It sounded the whole gamut of emotions: joyous gaiety, gripping love scenes, tragedy, revenge, and undying devotion. ... Crowds gathered before the doors were opened and thronged the entrance at the street. Practically everyone attending was in Spanish costume in keeping with the stage settings and costumes. The scene was like a leaf taken from an album of the days of 49."

WWI

After hearing that the German army had devastated Belgium in 1914, Charles Caldwell Park called the *Morning Press* and said, "Please don't ever again designate my home by the German name it has borne until now; call it Tipperary!" Park's sentiments were echoed nationwide as hamburger became Salisbury steak and sauerkraut became "Victory Cabbage." So *Tipperary* it was, after the name of the British anthem sung by soldiers heading to the front, and so it remained thereafter.

The Parks were busy during the war years. When the ladies who frequented the café in Diehl's world-famous grocery store found their sanctuary overtaken by rowdies from the Flying A Studio, Mrs. Park proposed forming a social club so she and her friends would have a place to meet for lunch, check parcels, leave messages, play cards, and read and write letters.

Left to right: Mrs. Levison Taylor (Maria de la Guerra), Lillian Taylor holding Maria Ealand, Kate Stow Ealand, Uncle Charles L. Taylor, director of the Carnegie Corporation Hero Fund, and Sally Taylor Alexander circa 1906-07. It was here at the Taylor home on Chapala Street that Helen Park, Sally, and Julia Redington Wilson created the Little Town Club. (Montecito Association History Committee)

Two rooms of the Orella Adobe on State Street, which was being used as a grocery store, were rented out to become the first home of the Little Town Club.

Helen Park, Julia Redington Wilson and Sally Taylor Alexander (later Stow) met at Sally's mother's home and decided to invite 20 friends to join the club. They initially rented two rooms in the 1859 Orella Adobe where Lawrence Orella operated a small grocery store. (This building was remodeled to become the Copper Coffee Pot and then Aldo's near the corner of Figueroa and State streets.) Today's Little Town Club, as it came to be called, stands near the corner of Carrillo and Anacapa streets.

In January 1917, Helen Park convinced the city council to launch the Santa Barbara Free Market, whose expenses she underwrote. Built on the property of Neighborhood House, the covered market faced Santa Barbara Street and was open on all sides. According to a newspaper account of the day, Mrs. Park's goal was "to bring producers and consumers closer together," in the hope of reducing the

Public Market!

Santa Barbara and De la Guerra Sts.

Open
Tuesdays, Thursdays, Saturdays

Beginning
TODAY
7 a. m. — 1 p. m.

For information telephone Santa Barbara 13—both phones.

Helen Park founded the Public Market, a precursor of today's farmers markets, on the property of the Neighborhood House.

price of food for some in the community and bringing needed income to others. Thirty-two tables rented for 15 cents a day and the ground was neatly padded with wood chips donated by the mill. The market hoped to include not only vegetables, flowers and plants, but also cakes, eggs and chickens.

It's a Long Way to Tipperary

Nineteen hundred and seventeen saw ramped up community efforts at war relief work. Knitting clubs, like the Mariposa knitting club, which met at the home of Mrs. Higginson on Channel Drive, had sprung up throughout the city. Men and women volunteered at the Red Cross headquarters in town to knit woolen hoods and afghans and create surgical dressings. Dozens of fund-raisers for the war effort were in the works throughout the area.

It must have been a bit of a shock, therefore, when the

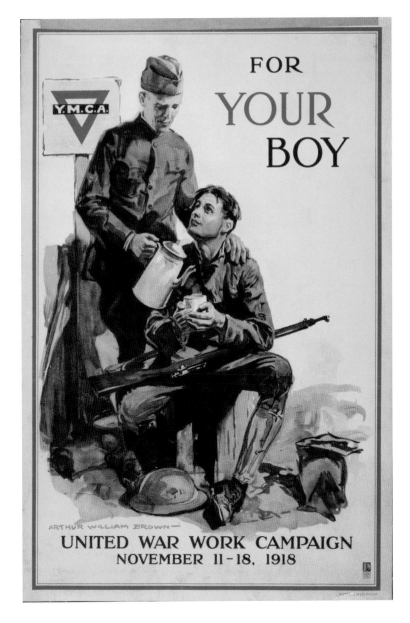

FOR YOUR BOY

Y.M.C.A.

ARTHUR WILLIAM BROWN

UNITED WAR WORK CAMPAIGN
NOVEMBER 11-18, 1918

During WWI, American artists went to work to recruit funds and volunteers to help with the war effort at home and abroad. (Courtesy Library of Congress)

Morning Press announced the departure of the community-minded Park family for an indefinite period of time. The public was not informed, at first, that Dr. and Mrs. Park and daughters Nancy and Elizabeth were not planning to stay in New York but instead had taken out passports for

England and France. Their stated purpose was to finance a home for convalescent soldiers and to purchase hospital supplies.

By January 1918, these plans had morphed into the creation of a YMCA canteen named Old Fort Duquesne Café in Tours, France. Located near six American Expeditionary Forces cantonments, the canteen served meals to 1,700 to 2,000 soldiers each day. The Harrisburg, Pennsylvania *Evening News* said Dr. Park had named the canteen in honor of his native city. Park had convinced the YMCA, said the report, that there was a demand for a restaurant that served American-style food with none of the "oo-la-la touches" of the French. "Boys in olive drab want grub, not cuisine," the writer opined.

Upon his return to Santa Barbara in August 1918, Dr. Park told the *Morning Press* that the canteen was "a great, big happy place where the American soldiers can smoke, chum with each other, and all in all enjoy a respite from the arduous duties of army life."

"Loneliness is one thing that gets the American soldier," continued Park, "That is where the YMCA is being felt. These soldier boys, thrown in a strange country, far from home where an unknown tongue is spoken, hunger for their own countrymen, and long for the sight and voice of an American girl."

Dr. Park had been ordered by his doctors to take a much-needed rest outside of Europe, so the family had sailed back to the United States, but he and his daughters were planning to return that October. Through his persistence, Dr. Park had been able to secure sugar and coal and other needed commodities for the American soldiers though he

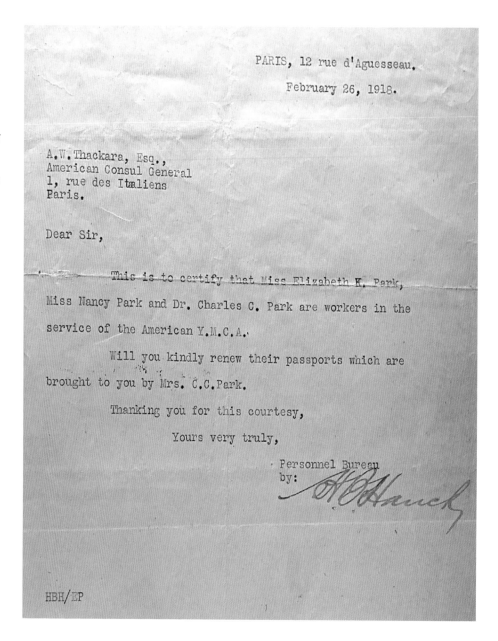

Letter requesting a renewal of passports for the Parks.

credited the financing by his friends for the success of his efforts.

Two other Santa Barbarans had joined the Parks at the canteen. One was Charles W. Dabney, real estate broker and owner of the Ontare Ranch, who was part of the consular Dabney family who had settled in the Azores in 1867. Dabney had worked diligently during the

Local heroes, Jane McLaren, Charles Caldwell Park, Nancy Park, and Elizabeth Park applied for passports to help set up a YMCA canteen in Tours, France.

war years with the local Red Cross, YMCA, and two Liberty Loan drives and heeded Dr. Park's call for help with the canteen in Tours.

The second, "Aunt" Jane McLaren, was one of the daughters of a Presbyterian minister who had retired to Santa Barbara in the 1870s. She was prominent in social causes such as the founding of Cottage Hospital and the St. Cecelia Club, which funded a free bed at the hospital for those who could not afford care, as well as such community events as the Flower Festivals. Jane traveled to Tours to help with the Café and stayed for another year after the armistice because she felt there so much more to do. Her 1921 *Morning Press* obituary said, "Though she was no longer young, her spirit was keen and she worked far harder than many of the young girls over there."

When Dr. Park spoke of Dabney and McLaren's work, reported the *Press*, "his kind eyes smiled a beaming approval of their splendid cooperation."

In the end, the Parks did not return to France. When the war ended on November 11, 1918, Dr. Park became head of the committee that greeted the returning soldiers to Santa Barbara.

Dr. Charles Caldwell Park made his final departure from Santa Barbara on August 14, 1931, at his home in Montecito after an illness of several weeks. Helen followed in 1935. Together, they left a legacy of community service and organizations that continue to affect and enrich the community today.

Adele and Albert Herter at Près Choisis *aka* The Creeks, *their estate in the Hamptons, circa 1940*

Albert and Adele

Born in 1871, Albert Herter was a son of Christian Augustus Ludwig Herter of Stuttgart, who, together with his half-brother Gustav, had formed Herter Brothers, the leading cabinetmaking and interior design company of New York during the Gilded Age. His mother, Mary Miles Herter, was the daughter of a prominent East Coast physician. She had devoted her life to advancing the cause of Aestheticism, an artistic movement that promoted Beauty as the basic object of life.

With a life infused with art and beauty, it was no wonder that by age 14 Albert exhibited for the first time at the Academy of Fine Arts in New York City. He studied at the Art Students League and painted his first mural at age 15. His widowed mother took him on a world tour the following year.

In Paris it was decided that he should study independently under the personal supervision of the best artists rather than attend the École des Beaux Arts. In the early days, he was a protégé of Jean-Paul Laurens, a French painter in the Academic tradition who painted numerous large public works, and Fernand Corman, known mostly for history paintings and large decorative works. Their influence is clearly visible in Herter's genre and style.

When he was 18, Albert's *The Wife of Buddha* was accepted for the Paris Salon. Winning third place, it also won a buyer. When he was 22, he became engaged to fellow art student Adele L. McGinnis.

Born in 1869 in New York City, Adele was the daughter of prominent banker John W. McGinnis and Lydia Olivia Matteson McGinnis. Between 1888 and 1891, she was studying art in Paris with Bouguereau, Robert-Fleury, and Courtois when she met Albert.

The two returned to New York for an April 1893 wedding ceremony at St. Thomas's Church where Adele was whisked

Mary Miles Herter was a devotee of Aestheticism and a supporter of music concerts in Santa Barbara between 1904 and 1913.

down the aisle in an empire-style gown of white bengaline silk. With a wreath of orange blossoms securing a flowing tulle veil, Adele appeared to have stepped out of a Pre-Raphaelite painting. An overflowing bouquet of Easter lilies completed the Aesthetic effect.

Immediately afterward, the newlyweds caught a train for Chicago where Albert's work was on display at the

Albert's The Round Mirror *shows his propensity for the Pre-Raphaelite style.*

Early Artistic Life

Albert had first visited Japan during his world tour at age 16. Shortly after their honeymoon, Albert and Adele returned to the Land of the Rising Sun to live for several years. In a 1904 interview he said, "I found Japan a Garden of Eden. It impressed me as being the most beautiful country in the whole world."

Japan influenced the couple's art and lifestyle, and Albert took to wearing a kimono and hakama in Japan as well as in his Paris studio. Adele's portraits and still-life paintings always included elements of Japanese decorative arts.

In 1899, the estate called *Près Chosis* (aka *The Creeks*), which the couple had commissioned to be built in the Hamptons, was completed. The house boasted two artists' studios in addition to a host of elegant rooms, which were suffused with color.

The formal gardens of Près Choisis *exuded a palette of rich colors.*
(Library of Congress)

Chicago World's Fair of 1893. From there it was a race to San Francisco to board a steamer for Japan for their year-long honeymoon.

Upon their return, the Art Institute of Chicago hosted an exhibition of both artists' watercolors on Japanese subjects.

Adele's still-life shows her liking of warm tones and floral themes.

"The hands of Pryderi and Rhiannon were held fast by the enchanted bowl, and their feet by the enchanted slab; and their joyousness forsook them, and they could not utter a word." (Tales of the Enchanted Islands of the Atlantic)

The Herters didn't return to the United States permanently until 1904. In February 1908, Adele and Albert established Herter Looms in Mary Herter's former Madison Avenue home. Utilizing weavers from France and a talented crew of artists to create designs and tapestries, the looms were the first to make use of synthetic silk, a precursor to nylon.

Adele became known for her portraits, still-life paintings,

and decorative murals. Her work was exhibited in many New York galleries over the years and her portraits include some of the better-known names of high society in the early part of the twentieth century. Her life-size painting of Albert in Japanese dress was selected for the Salon in Paris. Japan's influence showed clearly in her work and one reviewer wrote, "The painter uses Oriental objects very cleverly for backgrounds, obtaining low but rich color effects."

Albert became renowned for monumental murals of historic and allegorical scenes, romantic portraits, and decorative arts. He was also a widely published illustrator whose photogravures appeared in such magazines as *Harper's Bazaar* and in several novels such as *Tales of the Enchanted Islands of the Atlantic (1899)* by Thomas Wentworth Higginson and *The Grandissimes* (1907) by George W. Cables.

Albert's murals hang in public buildings throughout the nation, his paintings and tapestries adorn the galleries of the world's art museums, and the list of medals and honors he was awarded is extensive.

The Road to Santa Barbara

The Herters' presence in Santa Barbara dates to 1904, when Albert's mother Mary purchased an entire city block bounded by Micheltorena, Garden, Anacapa and Arrellaga streets and commissioned designs for an Italianate villa. In 1909, Albert and Adele came to Santa Barbara to help her decorate her home.

Mary settled into her villa across from Alameda Park and became involved in the artistic life of the community. She opened her home for fundraisers and assisted in organizing Italian fetes at Oak Park for band benefits. She also helped bring to town the fiery Italian composer and conductor, Caesar La Monaca, to organize outdoor concerts. On concert

Albert in the courtyard at El Mirasol (Photo by Carolyn and Edwin Gledhill)

days at Alameda Park, there was always space left for Madame Herter's carriage from which she could listen to the concert in comfort.

When Mary died suddenly in March 1913, Albert inherited her home. Beginning to tire of the nomadic life they

Published For Nye Sight Seeing Autos, Santa Barbara, Cal.

Mary Miles Herter helped bring to town the fiery Caesar La Monaca (third from left) to give outdoor concerts.

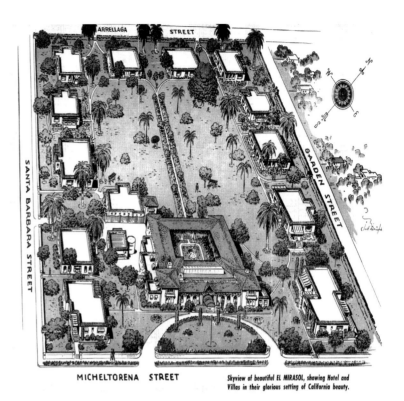

El Mirasol sat on an entire downtown block and boasted several bungalows set amidst a horticultural wonderland of rare and exotic plantings.

had been living, the couple decided to turn Mary's home into an exclusive hotel and open a California showroom for Herter Looms. They also established a studio at 114 Chapala Street and at other addresses over the years. From 1927-1929, Adele had a space at the Meridian Studios, and Albert is reputed to have used a studio in the 300 block of Canon Perdido Street.

El Mirasol

Albert and Adele renovated Mary's home into an exclusive hotel by building 15 bungalows, planting exquisite gardens, and lavishing the interior with unique artistry. They held a contest asking Santa Barbarans to name the new hotel, and the name *El Mirasol* won out. Catering to the elite of the Gilded Age, El Mirasol advertised itself as the hotel of choice for those "who dislike the publicity, the noise and promiscuity of a large hotel…. There will be no band, no ill-mannered and indifferent bell boys, no obligatory tipping

at every turn to insure attention." Instead, the brochure stated, "one will find a pervasive spirit of quiet cordiality and cheerfulness."

At the opening on August 18, 1914, a local reporter sang its praises by writing, "Everywhere is color, harmonious tones that are felt as well as seen; rich rugs, hangings, pictures, pottery, and lightshades of exceptional loveliness, so finely wrought that each is a masterpiece of its kind."

Among the many artistic elements Albert created for the hotel were two panels depicting peacocks, the colorful bird associated with the Aesthetic Movement. The murals hung above bold orange and blue flooring in the smaller dining room, which became known as the Peacock Room.

Adele patiently ironed silver foil wrapping from Chinese tea packages and affixed them to the wall of the room that

Mary Herter's home became El Mirasol Hotel in 1914.

El Mirasol brochures promised guests a "pervasive spirit of quiet cordiality and cheerfulness."

was later to become the bar. Upon this reflective canvas she painted desert scenes depicting all manner of cacti. When Frank Lloyd Wright visited, he exclaimed that it was the most beautiful wall covering he had ever seen. In 1931, Adele reprised her cactus design for the dining room of Amy du Pont's Montecito estate, *Casa del Sueno.*

The Herters sold El Mirasol to San Francisco hotelier Frederick Clift in 1920, but by then they were well ensconced in Santa Barbara's artistic life and had adopted the community as their own.

One of the El Mirasol bungalows set in the colorful garden.

Frank Lloyd Wright told Adele that her cactus murals were the most beautiful wall coverings he had ever seen.

A section of Adele's re-creation of the cactus mural for Amy du Pont's home, Casa del Sueno

The Herter Touch in California

Though Albert and Adele continued to travel and spend part of the year at *The Creeks,* their art began to reflect the influence of the West.

Their son Christian A. Herter, who became Secretary of State under President Eisenhower, recalled springtime gatherings when the family motored through a California countryside ablaze with yellow-gold poppies. The rich colors and flowers of the West entered the Herters' palette and found exuberant expression in their work.

Albert became increasingly involved with California commissions. In 1913 Albert created seven murals entitled *The Pageant of the Nations* for the Mural Room of the St. Francis Hotel in San Francisco. In 1928, he painted eight history murals for the Los Angeles Public Library. The one entitled *Fiesta at a Mission* features Mission Santa Barbara. When he was criticized for inaccurately depicting the Indians in feather headdresses of the Great Plains, he is said to have retorted, "Madame, those are visiting Indians!"

One of seven murals Herter created for the St. Francis Hotel in San Francisco

In Santa Barbara, Albert and Adele's paintings found their way into the homes of such local notables as Bernard Hoffmann, Pearl Chase, W. Edwin Gledhill, and Kathleen Burke Peabody Hale. Albert also completed two of 10 proposed murals for his *History of Writing* series for the Santa Barbara Public Library. His *The Gutenberg Bible* (1944) and *Egyptian Hieroglyphics* (1935) still hang in their place of honor in the

Albert's Egyptian Hieroglyphs *still enhances the main lobby of the central branch of the Santa Barbara Public Library.*

Establishing Community Traditions

*I*n 1920, Adele Herter took up the effort spearheaded by Pearl Chase to create a community Christmas program. Utilizing the tallest evergreen tree on the County Courthouse property, both Herters set about creating ornaments, designing costumes, and laying plans. A red-robed chorus of 100 voices was to carry golden lanterns on long poles as

The first Tree of Light stood on the property of the old County Courthouse.

main room of the downtown branch of the library

In the 1920s Albert served as an instructor at the newly-formed Santa Barbara School of the Arts and often showed up with dramatic flair in a colorful red fox-hunting coat. One of his students, Gordon Kenneth Grant, worked with him on the *America the Beautiful* murals, which were financed by Caroline Hazard of Mission Canyon for Wellesley College where she had been dean. Grant went on to become a noted muralist in his own right.

In 1929, Albert and Adele were recruited by Bernard Hoffmann to decorate the Gold Room, part of the Anacapa Addition to his El Paseo restaurant. They designed rich gold and red draperies to be woven at Herter Looms, painted frescoes, created poppy-gold hangings, and painted gilded-poppy designs on the ceiling beams.

The Community Arts String Orchestra, conducted by Georges (Roger) Clerbois, played their early concerts on the stage of the Recreation Center. Herter Looms created the curtains seen in the background, and Adele designed the musicians' costumes.

they wended their way along the courthouse paths to the Christmas Tree.

In an interview several weeks before the event, Adele expressed the hope that the Community Christmas Celebration would become an annual event that was anticipated joyously each year. "We want it to be more than gifts and good cheer," she said. "We want to feed their souls as well as their bodies."

On Christmas Eve, however, the threat of imminent rain sent the whole performance to the Recreation Center. Though it was too crowded to allow everyone inside, the show did go on. A series of three tableaux, directed by Adele, were accompanied by the singing of Christmas carols. The final tableau, which resembled an old Italian painting, depicted the *Madonna and Child with Angels*. The chorus and audience accompanied the tableaux by singing "Silent Night."

The *Morning Press* reviewer said that despite the fact that much of the effect was lost due to the cramped quarters, "it is improbable that Santa Barbara has ever before seen stage setting, grouping, and costuming so exquisitely designed and executed…. Those who were fortunate enough both to see and hear received impressions that will remain long with them."

The Tree of Light (as it came to be called), choral program, and *tableaux vivant* became a regular part of the community celebration for many years. A year after the earthquake and subsequent reconstruction of the County Courthouse, a tree at the destroyed Arlington Hotel became the Community Christmas Tree until 1928, when the Norfolk Island Pine on the corner of Carrillo and Chapala streets received that designation, one that persists to this day, a legacy from Pearl Chase and the Herters.

In 1920, Albert and Adele Herter became involved with founding the Community Arts Association (CAA), which brought the various elements of Santa Barbara's cultural life under one umbrella. Adele served on the board of directors, and in 1921, she became a founder and chairwoman of the Music Branch of CAA. She had a plan for a two-year concert program and assigned other members to various subcommittees, such as publicity (Kathleen Burke Peabody), finance (Pearl Chase), and programs (Florence Fernald).

In 1922, Adele Herter joined with Pearl Chase, Bernhard Hoffmann and several others of the Community Arts Association's Drama Branch to restore the old Lobero Theatre. (When the original building was deemed too compromised to retrofit, it was replaced.)

Promoting Community Aesthetics

Albert's artistic and dramatic bents found outlet with the Community Arts Players. Besides acting and directing, he designed costumes, scenery and stage curtains. The Potter Theater received a gold curtain, and the Recreation Center received a gold and "Herter blue" curtain that was later used at the Lobero Theatre; both were woven at Herter Looms.

By far the most renowned performance of 1921 was Albert's staging of Maurice Maeterlinck's dark fairytale of doomed lovers, *Pelléas and Mélisande*. Albert played the role of Golaud, Mélisande's husband and Pelléas' brother. The beautiful and elaborate performance with its incredible scenery and costuming designed by Albert and direction by Nina Moise, a well-respected director of the day, left a lasting impression on the community.

Herter, who was roundly applauded for his role, nevertheless was tripped up on opening night. He had been

Albert's artistic and dramatic nature led him to revel in designing and wearing elaborate costumes like his rendition of the Byzantine emperor Justinian. (Library of Congress)

told that all of Hollywood was in the audience, and a sudden case of the jitters caused him to forget his lines. He had to say to the audience, "I don't know what I am saying," and walk to the wings where the book holder gave him his lines.

His break from character didn't seem to overly affect the performance, for the *Morning Press* reviewer, overcome by

1923—FOURTH ANNUAL SEASON—1924

COMMUNITY ARTS PLAYERS
PRESENT

KING SOLOMON
BY
IRA REMSEN

PRODUCED BY ALBERT HERTER
DIRECTED BY NINA MOISE
MUSIC BY ARTHUR BLISS

POTTER THEATRE   FRIDAY EVENING, MARCH 21,
SANTA BARBARA   SATURDAY AFTERNOON AND
CALIFORNIA   EVENING, MARCH 22.

Playbill for King Solomon

As early as 1909, Albert was involved in creating dramatic tableaux like this scene which was included in The Temple. *As in Santa Barbara, Albert played the role of Dionysius in this earlier tableau. (Library of Congress)*

the magic and romance of it all, wrote, "[It was] a midwinter night's dream told by the flickering light of the dying fire that throws haunting shadows upon the walls and wakes the figures in the tapestries who stir and whisper they were once men and women from Fairyland, long, long ago. And then we listen while a pair of lovers tell us how they lived and died, and how there was a castle by the sea."

In April 1922, Albert created and produced the first original production given by the Community Arts Players, *The Temple.* Dubbing it a Greek pantomime, Herter designed the costumes and sets and co-directed with Nina Moise. Consisting of a series of *tableaux vivant* accompanied by the music of Georges (later Roger) Clerbois and the Community Arts Orchestra, the effect was like listening to a concert while

viewing a series of ever-changing masterpieces of art.

"*The Temple* is a feast of Beauty and Inspiration," wrote *Morning Press* reviewer Sarah Redington. "Never has aesthetic art been more truly served than in this dream of an artist who shows the soul of ancient Greece."

A cast of more than 100 appeared as torchbearers and flower maidens, fruit bearers, and warriors with golden shields and helmets. Ynez de la Guerra Dibblee performed exotic dances. Adele and Albert's grandson, Everit Herter, played Little Faun, and Fanny Oliver of *Rocky Nook* played Grandmother. Albert himself was Dionysius, surrounded by bacchantes wearing leopard skins and grape wreaths twined in their curls.

While Adele continued to serve on various boards of the

Community Arts Association, Albert produced one more play at the Potter Theater. For the production of *King Solomon*, he cast himself in the austere role of Zodak, Solomon's high priest. In 1925, the Santa Barbara earthquake destroyed the Potter Theater and it was not rebuilt. By then, Albert and Adele had returned to Paris where Albert had been asked to paint a mural for the railway terminal of Gare de l'Est.

Gare de L'Est

Albert and Adele had three children. Christian Archibald Herter, their second son, was named for several generations of Christian Herters. He became governor of Massachusetts and Secretary of State under Dwight D. Eisenhower. Their other son, Everit, followed in his parents' footsteps and became an artist, and their daughter Lydia, also an artist, lived most of her life in Santa Barbara.

During World War I, Albert volunteered for the war effort by creating several war posters recruiting volunteers and soliciting donations for organizations like the YMCA and the Red Cross. His son Everit, a budding portraitist and decorative artist, joined the camouflage section of the Engineer Corps along with other notable artists of the day. Everit was among the troops who departed Paris from Gare de l'Est in June of 1918 for Château-Thierry and Belleau Wood. By the end of that month, U.S. forces suffered 9,777 casualties, of which 1,811 were fatal. Among the fatalities was Everit Herter.

In 1926, Albert painted a 27-foot-high, forty-foot-wide memorial for the Paris train station entitled *The Departure of Troops from Gare de l'Est*. The French government gave him a room in Versailles in which to paint the monumental tribute for which he was awarded the Chevalier Legion of Honor. At the emotional unveiling, applauding soldiers sat on top of trains that were backed into the station for the ceremony.

Lydia and Adele Herter circa 1903

Albert painted the image of his son Everit looking through a foggy train window and included his son Christian, his daughter Lydia, her friend and companion Ingeborg Praetorius, Adele, several grandchildren, and himself in the painting.

Adele Herter died in 1946 at their East Hampton estate and Albert came to live at El Mirasol in Santa Barbara. After he died in 1950, his daughter Lydia and her companion, Ingeborg Praetorius, arranged for a memorial exhibit of her parents' work. Many Santa Barbara and Montecito families loaned paintings to the exhibit at the Santa Barbara Museum of Art.

Locally, the Herters' work can still be seen at the Santa

The Departure of Troops from Gare de l'Est *hangs in a place of honor at the Paris train station*

Barbara Public Library, and on the ceiling of the current restaurant inhabiting the space that was once known as the Gold Room of the El Paseo Restaurant. The Lobero Theater, the Cactus Room at *Casa del Sueno*, the Community Arts Musical Association (CAMA) and the tradition of the Tree of Light remain as manifestations of the Herters' influence on the cultural and artistic life of Santa Barbara.

Albert Herter painted himself into the mural at Gare de l'Est. He is the man holding the flowers, clutching his heart and looking at a woman in pink, who is most likely Adele. She, in turn, is looking at the faint, blurred face of the soldier on the train, an image of her son who died at Château-Thierry.

La Fiesta de la Cuesta (*Gift of Jean Storke Menzies and Margaret Cox to Santa Barbara Historical Museum*)

Alexander Harmer: Painter of Spanish California

In the painting, *La Fiesta de la Cuesta,* Micaela Cota de la Cuesta deals *monte* under a grape arbor to an avid group of caballeros. Vaqueros corral horses in the background, and two mischievous boys sample *aguardiente* from a barrel and spit a stream of the burning liquid at a dog. Just as Pieter Brueghel the Elder brought 16th century Dutch peasant life to light, Alexander Harmer's brush breathed life into the tales and lifestyle of the early Californios. Kevin Starr, former California State Historian, wrote, "Joyous, colorful, well-researched, action-packed, Harmer's canvases of Old California filled out in visual terms the Santa Barbara legend."

Today, Rancho La Vega, Dr. Ramon de la Cuesta's 1850s ranch across the Santa Ynez River from Buellton, is a working winery. Grapevines still cover the slopes, and the old adobe, though much altered, still stands as living reminder of times long past, a past chronicled by Harmer.

Alexander Francis Harmer trod a long, winding road before landing in Santa Barbara to find his ultimate artistic destiny. Born in Newark, New Jersey, in 1856, he was the second-born of nine children. His father worked as a jappaner, applying a Japanese-style varnish to furnishings. His grandfather was a Methodist minister.

Alexander showed an interest in art at a very young age, and sold his first amateurish painting for two dollars to a kind neighbor when he was only 11 years old. Inspired by this largess, the young lad determined to become a painter of the West. For two years he worked as a messenger boy at a telegraph office in Newark until he'd saved enough money to leave home. In 1869, he made it as far west as Lincoln, Nebraska, and his subsequent experiences in the Midwest helped shape the man and the artist.

Alexander Harmer stands before the oft-painted and photographed portal of the Yorba-Abadie Adobe, which once stood on De la Guerra Plaza.

Many years later, Harmer's eldest daughter Inez recounted, "When Papa came West as a lad of 13 or 14, he worked at whatever he could to find employment. His association with the theater made him intimately familiar with all of Sullivan's operettas. He sang to us from *H.M.S. Pinafore, The Mikado*…. It was a lovely soft voice that we loved."

Harmer bounced around Kansas for some three years, working and sketching the Western scenes before him. Deciding he needed a more formal education in art, he made an unsuccessful attempt to enroll in the Pennsylvania Academy of the Fine Arts. With money scarce but his ambition strong, he lied about his age and enlisted in the army. He finally made it to the Far West when he joined Company B, of the First U.S. Cavalry Regiment, which was stationed at Benicia Barracks in California.

Although he had listed his occupation as painter, he was appointed hospital steward, an indication that perhaps his commanding officers suspected he was underage. For a time he was also posted at Halleck, Nevada, where he surely experienced a wilder West than the fort on San Francisco Bay. After a year of saving his meager pay, he requested and received a discharge so he could return to Philadelphia to attend the Pennsylvania Academy of the Fine Arts.

The Road to Santa Barbara

Reaching Philadelphia in 1874, Harmer still didn't have enough money for school, so he acquired work as a photographer's assistant and spent his free time painting and sketching. Eventually, a trio of influential artists recognized his talent and arranged for his acceptance into the art academy. One of these was the controversial Thomas Eakins, realist painter and photographer, who stressed close observation of nature and a mathematical approach

Harmer drew many illustrations for Outing Magazine, *like this one for John C. Bourke's 1885 series entitled, "With General Crook in the Sierra Madre."*

Geronimo (center) with General Nelson A. Miles (to his left) at the 1901 Pan-America Exposition (World's Fair) in Buffalo, New York. Geronimo was captured for the final time in 1886 under Miles' command. (Library of Congress)

to composition. Harmer studied under Eakins and the two became great friends.

In 1876, Harmer left the Academy of Fine Arts but stayed in Philadelphia to work and paint on his own. During much of this time, he was living with a married sister and her husband. His widowed mother was also part of the household.

Then on September 2, 1881, Harmer again felt the call of the West. He re-enlisted in the army as a private in Troop L of the Sixth Cavalry and headed for Fort Apache, Arizona. During this time, he kept up a correspondence with Eakins, who sent him a camera to help with his studies of western landscapes, army life, and especially the Indians.

For the next 10 years, Harmer's adventures led him back and forth between the West and the East. In 1883, he asked General George Crook if he could join the field expedition that was following the renegade Apache, Geronimo, into Old Mexico. Harmer was present when Geronimo was captured for the third, but not the final, time.

The beautiful and charming Felicidad Abadie soon captured Harmer's heart.

This expedition and others provided Harmer with material for paintings of Native American life. Many of his illustrations began appearing in national magazines such as *Harper's Weekly*, as well as in Captain John Bourke's book, *An Apache Campaign in the Sierra Madre*. One of Harmer's finest paintings during this time was *Bringing in the Renegade, Geronimo*.

Years later, Alexander took his wife and daughter Inez to the 1901 World's Fair in Buffalo, New York. There, Geronimo was presiding over the Indian Congress and Village Exhibition. The passage of time and romanticization of his exploits had granted him celebrity status. "He was ever so glad to see Papa," Harmer's daughter said later, "and shook hands with us all, even giving me his card on which he had printed his name."

After Harmer's adventure with the hunt for Geronimo, he moved back and forth between stints at the Pennsylvania Academy of the Fine Arts and explorations of the West, including a period spent sketching and painting the

By the time Harmer arrived in California, most of the missions lay in ruins. Harmer drew them as they appeared in their glory days. The drawing above depicts the 1835 funeral of Governor José Figueroa, who is buried in the crypt at the Santa Barbara Mission.

California missions. At some point, Harmer met up with Charles Fletcher Lummis, a multifaceted and eccentric genius, who in 1884 had walked to California from Cincinnati, Ohio, to take a reporter job at the *Los Angeles Times*.

In 1891, Lummis, who besides being a journalist was a photographer and avid historical preservationist, invited Harmer to join him at the Del Valle family's Rancho Camulos, the ranch used as the setting for Helen Hunt Jackson's famous novel, *Ramona*.

Here, Harmer witnessed historic family re-enactments, which Lummis photographed, and, here, he was introduced to the daughter of Maria del Refugio and Dominque Abadie of Santa Barbara, the beautiful and charming Felicidad. Harmer was smitten.

Santa Barbara

On August 2, 1893, *The Daily Independent* announced that Ygnacio Ramón del Valle of Rancho Camulos was staying at the Commercial Hotel. That afternoon, in a small ceremony attended only by family and intimate friends, Alexander and Felicidad were married at the residence of Reverend Father James Villa of Our Lady of Sorrows Church. The Reverend Father Ferrer performed the ceremony, Felicidad's brother was best man, and Miss Isabel del Valle of Camulos was bridesmaid. The newlyweds caught the afternoon train for San Francisco, where Harmer had a studio, and where they would live for several months while Harmer settled his affairs.

The following year, the Harmers returned to Santa Barbara to live in the Yorba-Abadie Adobe, Felicidad's girlhood home. Harmer opened a studio in the Clock Building at 934½ State Street, Room 28, before moving it to the Hawley Block at 1229½ State Street. His first known work in Santa Barbara was the cover for the 1895 Flower Festival booklet.

Harmer's first Santa Barbara commission was the floral festival brochure.

Over the years, Harmer would have many such bread-and-butter commissions. He produced a series of calendar covers for Show and Hunt's grocery business and continued illustrating for magazines such as Lummis' *The Land of Sunshine.*

He also created illustrations for books such as *A Plaything of the Gods,* the story of Joaquin Murieta, by Carl Gray (aka Dr. C. C. Park); Father Zephyrin Engelhardt's books on the missions of California; and Santa Barbara lawyer Jarrett T. Richards' *Romance on El Camino Real.* California school children were introduced to Harmer's artistry through their readers. The Arlington Hotel commissioned menu covers and placemats, and Show and Hunt ordered mission scenes

Harmer designed the decorations for the admiral's carriage and painted the scene of the parade and Battle of the Flowers celebrating the visit of the Great White Fleet in 1908. (Gift of Glen and Louise Idleman to Santa Barbara Historical Museum)

for porcelain plates executed by Wedgwood of England.

About 1900, U.S. Attorney-General Philander Knox commissioned Harmer to create a frieze for the library of his estate in Pittsburg. It contained 50 embossed and painted leather panels, totaling 350 square feet, portraying images of all the major Indian tribes in the nation. Harmer spent weeks at the Smithsonian Institution, sketching from photographs and artifacts the unique characteristics of each tribe. The project took 18 months to complete and assured Harmer's reputation in the East.

Harmer designed costumes and props for theater productions, such as Victor Herbert's ill-fated 1909 first-American opera, *Natoma*, the story of a Chumash heroine during mission

Harmer often used his family and friends as models for his paintings. The dancers in "Dancing in the Moonlight at Casa De la Guerra" may be based on photos taken by Charles Lummis of Felicidad dancing with Ramón del Valle.

All eyes are on the combatants in a wrestling match or faux bullfight in the center of the colorful crowd in this watercolor. Indian and pueblo women sell food and other goods from blankets spread on the ground. Certain recognizable figures recur in many of Harmer's paintings, including the Indian woman in the foreground of this one and the small dogs. (Courtesy Marlene and Warren Miller)

days in Santa Barbara. Though the critics liked the music, they felt that the opera was "cruelly handicapped by a preposterous libretto" which they found was "incredibly fatuous and inane." In 1916, Harmer both loaned historic clothing from the trunks of Santa Barbara's old Spanish families and designed costumes and properties for the three-hour "photo play" of *Ramona*, a film adaptation of Helen Hunt Jackson's famous novel.

In 1908, Harmer created two paintings of the visit of the Great White Fleet to Santa Barbara. He also designed the advertising poster and the decorations for the admiral's floral carriage. Inez later remembered helping her father decorate the carriage, attaching white chrysanthemums through a covering of chicken wire. All of the reins and trappings were covered with rich golden-yellow sateen, and he had designed the costumes of the drivers and outriders as well.

What Harmer became most famous for, however, were his representations of California life during the early 1800s. One writer said that Harmer "attempted to capture the fading memories of the old Spanish Days through his studies with the aid of the remaining pioneers."

His success with these paintings stemmed from his deep artistic empathy and understanding of the historic lifestyle. "Harmer," said one critic, "more than any other Western painter, invoked a feeling of serenity, a timelessness, and a humanitarian sensitivity to his subjects. When he switched his emphasis to studies and impressions of California life, his style became much more impressionistic as well."

This illustration for Jarrett T. Richards' Romance on El Camino Real *shows characters Carmelita and Pancho sitting in the window seat of a venerable adobe based on Casa de la Guerra. (Courtesy James Main Fine Art)*

Life in Santa Barbara

Harmer and Felicidad would raise seven children to adulthood at the Yorba-Abadie Adobe, which stood on De la Guerra Plaza next to today's City Hall. Their oldest daughter, Inez, remembers that her childhood was divided between their town home and their ranch in Santa Ynez, "with its adobe house, terraced garden and wildcats, mountain lions and bears stalking the shadows cast by the light from our windows." Many of Harmer's paintings were inspired by the landscape of the valley.

Alexander Harmer in his studio

The Yorba-Abadie-Harmer Adobe stood east of today's City Hall on De la Guerra Plaza.

"Once," said Inez in an undated interview with Rosario Curletti (another daughter of the dons), "we went to the Santa Ynez River, and in a meadow Papa found what he wanted and set up his umbrella and sketching paraphernalia. I took up my 22-rifle and began shooting squirrels. Suddenly, some cattle charged me! Papa was near a tree, and he called to me to climb it while he waved his umbrella at the stampeding herd and somehow managed to shoo them off."

In town, Harmer and his children loved walking the streetless countryside to visit friends or take in a polo match on the Westside field. At Christmas time, Harmer snuck a red-berried toyon bush into the house to use as a Christmas tree. Tree ornaments were empty eggshells on which he'd painted little scenes from the nativity.

"Whenever Mama had been to a concert, she would return to the old adobe, seat herself at the piano, and repeat

Inez Harmer Northrup stands before a portrait of herself at the Santa Barbara Historical Museum in the 1950s. Harmer painted her draped in a 100-year-old serape.

"Y qué santa es esta?"

the concert in toto," said Inez. "Almost always, people would stand outside on the veranda to listen, and if the weather was inclement, they would knock on the door and ask to come in." Invariably, she and her brother Bert would end the evening by dancing the cakewalk as everyone sang and her mother played the piano.

At the end of a porch of their adobe, Harmer had created a studio, which he had decorated with Indian baskets, saddles and other accoutrements of Californian life. "On the mantle," said Inez, "he had a bust of Venus di Milo and he always chuckled when he recalled the old paisano who looked a long time at her and then asked softly, *'Y qué santa es esta?'"* (And what saint is this one?)

"My favorite moments with him were in the garden as my mother and I watched with him the sunsets, the beautiful ends of the day with the tree shadows blending with the stumbling night," said Inez. "His Victorian ideas prevented him from showing any emotion. The only time I felt I could was when I put my hand in his as we sat together at eventide, the three of us in the quiet of the garden."

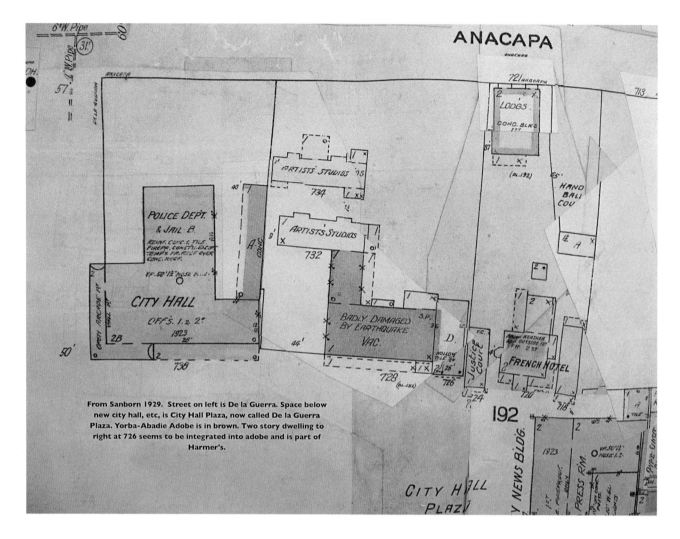

The 1929 Sanborn Fire Insurance Map shows the Harmer complex after the Santa Barbara earthquake. By this time, City Hall had replaced the Raffour House Hotel and two adobes.

From Sanborn 1929. Street on left is De la Guerra. Space below new city hall, etc, is City Hall Plaza, now called De la Guerra Plaza. Yorba-Abadie Adobe is in brown. Two story dwelling to right at 726 seems to be integrated into adobe and is part of Harmer's.

Establishing an Art Colony

*I*n 1906, contributing to the establishment of Santa Barbara as an artist's colony, Harmer built the second of two wooden studio duplexes; the first one adjoined his adobe. Already ensconced in a studio at Harmer's was Rob Wagner. Now with the completion of the second set of studios, Fernand Lungren and Henry M. Howard were to join them. In the McKay building across De la Guerra Plaza, Lockwood de Forest and Oscar Coast had studios.

By 1908, the *San Francisco Call* was able to publish an article entitled "The Artist Colony of Santa Barbara," listing the names and genres of the renowned artists who had made the city their home base. "Not far from the studio of Gamble and Davis," wrote the reporter, "is that of Alexander Harmer, which was for a long time the Bohemia of Santa Barbara, housing all the painters of the town." By 1909, the works of these Santa Barbara artists, including Harmer, were receiving high praise at the Seattle World's Fair.

Over the years, notable artists such as Clarence R. Mattei, Frederick Rhead, DeWitt Parshall, Colin Campbell Cooper, Adele Herter, Dudley Carpenter, Arthur Merton Hazard, Maynard Dixon, Carl Oscar Borg, Frederick Junior, Gilbert

Charles Lummis photographed Ethel and Helen Harmer with Ed Borein in front of the famous Harmer portal.

Harmer posed his daughters near the oft-painted and photographed portal of his adobe in order to paint two shyly flirtatious señoritas.

White, Ella S. Valk, John Marshall Gamble and many others leased day studios from Harmer.

In 1921, Ed Borein, who was already a famous painter of the West, and his wife Lucile were invited to live in one of these studios. Lucile wrote, "There is one very large room, a small kitchen, and Ed expects to build on another room for a bedroom. It will be rather small quarters, but I know we are going to get lots of fun out of it." (The Boreins spent a year before moving into larger accommodations.)

On January 10, 1925, Alexander Harmer died while admiring a sunset in his backyard. Ironically, that day he had received a "paper talk" (an illustrated letter) from friend Charles Russell, which said, "Here's hoping your trail is a long one, / Plain and easy to ride. / May your dry camps

Ed Borein (wearing a hat) with Lucile on his right in front of his studio at Harmer's.

Costumed Santa Barbara girls enact a scene, possibly for Fiesta of 1924, at the Harmer Adobe. All that remains of the complex today is this wavy wall.

be few, / and Health ride with you / to the pass on the big divide." Alexander crossed that pass just six months short of the Santa Barbara earthquake, which left the venerable adobe in ruins. Hopes of resuscitating it failed, and in 1945 it, too, followed Harmer across that Big Divide.

Alexander Harmer's works are an enduring and romantic historical record of Santa Barbara's Spanish roots. His long residency and intimate connections with the earlier culture imbued him with the spirit of Santa Barbara's early days, which he expressed after careful study and attention to historic detail through the development of his artistic genius.

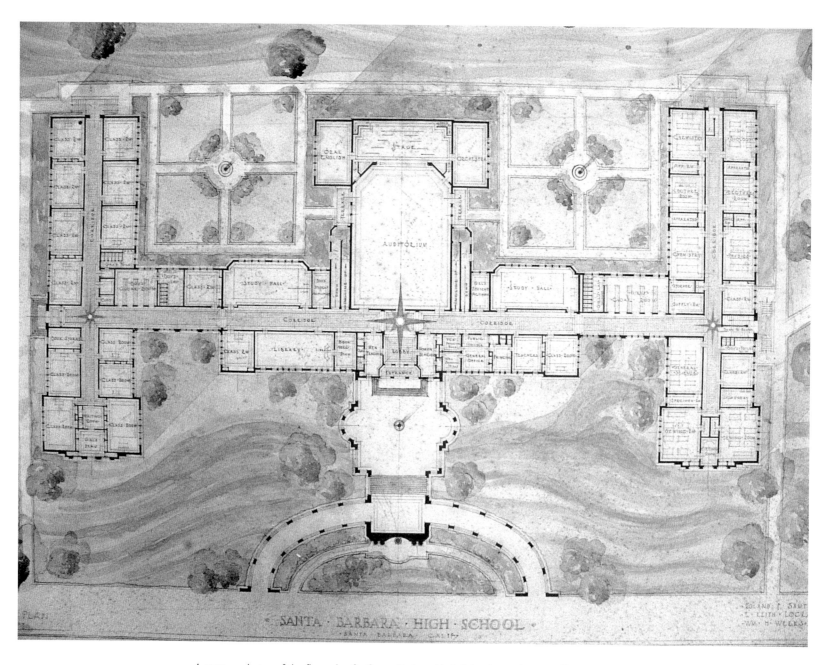

A 1922 rendering of the floor plan for Santa Barbara High School reveals its seriffed E-shape and the proposed uses for each space.

Roland Sauter, Santa Barbara Architect

Roland Frederic Sauter was one of Santa Barbara's premier architects, designing homes and structures in the Spanish tradition several years before George Washington Smith built his first Andalusian-influenced home in Montecito. Though his name is virtually unknown today, his works are an integral part of Santa Barbara's current architectural landscape.

Hailing from a humble Maryland farm family, Sauter studied art, design and drafting at the Maryland Institute for the Promotion of the Mechanic Arts, in the architectural department of the School of Design. He graduated in 1910. After a stint as a draftsman in Maryland and then in San Francisco, he came to Santa Barbara in 1912 and found work as foreman for the construction of *El Cerrito,* the Russell Ray/Windsor Soule-designed home for Clarence A. Black, one of the founders of Detroit's Cadillac Motor Company.

Black's Mission Revival style home was set high on a western-facing knoll of Mission Ridge. Writing in 1921, historian Michael Philips said that *El Cerrito* was supervised from foundation to last hammer stroke by Roland F. Sauter. Though the house itself was completed in 1914, Sauter continued to work for Clarence Black on various projects. These included grading Mountain Drive, Tremonto Road and Mission Ridge Road and supervising the construction of massive retaining walls that support the roads and surround the estate. Almost two miles of walls, some of which were four-feet-wide at their base and 30-feet-high with buttressed supports, were built.

Clearly an enthusiastic autoist, Clarence Black joined George Owen Knapp and other prominent local men in

Roland Sauter
circa 1920
(Courtesy of Rodney Sauter)

funding improvements to San Marcos Road, which was often closed to motorists. In May 1915, Sauter could be found in charge of six men and six horses as they graded curves, smoothed road beds, and improved drainage on the road.

Black was also an avid supporter of the Santa Barbara Mission and donated many improvements. In June 1915, he commissioned Sauter to design and supervise the construction of a wall to support the newly leveled grade of the parking lot in front of the Mission, repair the old reservoir, and rebuild an old stone wall. Sauter also designed a wait station for the Santa Barbara tramline on the corner of Laguna and Los Olivos streets. Utilizing native sandstone, the charming little station seated 30 people under its red-tiled roof, which

Sauter designed the tram wait station near the Mission.

was supported by six concrete colonnaded arches. (This wait station was demolished in the late 1960s/early '70s.)

In 1916, Sauter designed and built a mountain retreat for Clarence Black near San Marcos Pass. According to the *Daily News*, this lodge included an art studio and was used as a "weekend resting place and a place to entertain the friends of the family."

Sauter had opened an architectural office in the San Marcos Building on State Street in 1914. One of his first commissions came from the County of Santa Barbara

Sauter supervised the construction of Clarence Black's El Cerrito estate on Santa Barbara's Riviera and the stone walls that surround it.

Completed in 1918, the First Presbyterian Church incorporated touches of churrigueresque ornamentation and other features of Spanish Colonial architecture.

Sauter's 1916 rendering for the First Presbyterian Church on Anapamu Street

for a brick detention home at 1015 Garden Street. The simple flat-roofed, blockish building nevertheless exhibited some elegant detailing in a curving balustrade of the columned entryway and a patterned frieze.

In 1916, Roland was saving his pennies and living at the YMCA on the corner of Carrillo and Chapala streets. He bid for and received the commission to design the First Presbyterian Church across from the new Public Library on Anapamu Street. *The Morning Press* of June 1916 reported that his design, in the Spanish Renaissance tradition, was "fine and appropriate to this city." Sauter incorporated an arcaded cloister, balconies, a rose window, and a rotunda. The church ornamentation was simplified after the 1925 earthquake, but it stood thereafter unshaken until the city decided they wanted the site for a parking lot in the 1960s.

In 1918, Sauter presented a rendering for the Santa Barbara County National Bank on the corner of State and Carrillo streets. Heavily ornamented with churrigueresque embellishments, his design was passed over in favor of Myron Hunt's stripped-down architectural lines.

Graholm

In 1916, another Detroiter came to town and purchased a parcel of land on Constance Avenue within view of the mission and Clarence Black's *El Cerrito* estate. David Gray had helped Motor City earn its nickname by creating Gray Motor Company and representing his family's investment in the Ford Motor Company by serving on its board. Black, too, had been an investor with Ford, but they had parted ways early on. Undoubtedly, Clarence Black introduced Sauter to Gray, who hired the young architect and expressed a desire for a mission-inspired mansion.

Sauter convinced David Gray to change sites for his home. He had found an ideal parcel of 29 acres on Pepper Hill in Montecito with sweeping views of city, sea and mountain. Gray agreed and Sauter set to work in 1919. Careful not to disturb existing rocks or trees, Roland saw his design take form over the next 18 months as masons built foundations of stone laid in naturalistic patterns.

An intriguing labyrinth of a house, *Graholm* clearly granted Sauter full expression of his artistic genius. Revealing his artistry were rounded copper gutters running through the carved eaves, end cut wooden flooring, hand hewn beams and recessed detailing in the plaster above windows set into

The courtyard reveals Sauter's signature stonework design, classic fenestration, and wrought-iron grillwork and lighting fixtures.

The newly completed Graholm, with its winding drive, looks across Camino Viejo Road toward Frederick Forrest Peabody's Solana estate.

Sauter's design for Deer Lodge *made the most of spectacular views of the Santa Ynez Valley. (Courtesy of John Fritsche)*

massive walls. Sauter's designs for the wrought-iron grills, sconces, windows, and gates took workmen nearly seven years to complete. He also designed twin service quarters separated by a five-bay garage to the north of the entrance gates.

His experience at *El Cerrito* came into play as he graded a long, twisting driveway lined by stone walls. Sauter had developed a signature style with stonework. Rather than having the dressed sides face out, he faced them in, allowing the patina of the aged stones to create a naturalistic impression.

His efforts did not go unnoticed. In June 1921, the *Daily News* reported a visitor who said, "This house looks as though it has grown right out of the hill!" Sauter was pleased, for

that was the effect he had intended. The road, too, was much admired. Wrote the reporter, "Sauter swung it to the east, brought it up with a sort of double airplane swoop, twisted it around a huge rock at the front, and brought it to rest triumphantly between two other huge boulders in the rear."

David Gray later hired Sauter to design and build a mountain lodge just over the San Marcos Pass. He called it *Deer Lodge,* and it was, of course, built of stone.

During this time, Roland took out a building permit for his own home on Mission Ridge. In 1922 he married Norma D. "Marty" Martin, and the two moved into the Mission-Pueblo influenced home, which rose from naturally laid stone foundations and was floored with end-cut wooden tiles.

David Gray admired Mission-style architecture, and Sauter accommodated him with thick walls, arched recesses, heavy-beamed ceilings, tiled floors, and deep window seats at Deer Lodge. (Courtesy of John Fritsche)

Newlyweds Roland and Marty at the home he built on Mission Ridge across from El Cerrito. (Courtesy of Rodney Sauter)

Roland and Marty on their honeymoon circa 1922. (Courtesy of Rodney Sauter)

Success

Roland's reputation soared and around 1922, he made E. Keith Lockard, local boy and graduate of Berkeley's architectural school, a partner. Lockard had worked as a draftsman and later as an architect for Sauter, and the new firm became known as Sauter & Lockard.

In 1922 they won the bid for the design of Santa Barbara's new City Hall. The original Victorian-era City Hall, which once stood in the middle of De la Guerra Plaza, had received a Mission-Revival face lift in 1909, but apparently it was not enough to please civic improvers. Ten years later the Community Arts Association's Plans and Planting Committee decided that one of their first tasks was "to develop the design for a new City Hall and the much needed improvement of De la Guerra Plaza," which included clearing the "paltry City Hall" out of the center of the plaza. Sauter & Lockard's design won their approval.

The three-story building replaced the old Raffour Hotel, which was moved down the street, along with an old ship's cabin from the wreck of a Spanish ship, which over the years had been used as a store and a shoe-repair shop.

The design included many details of wood, marble, wrought iron and plasterwork, but estimates put the project over budget so the ornamentation was reserved for the exterior detailing and the middle floor of the building. The police department and jails were once housed downstairs and cloistered arches still cover the 10-foot sidewalk on De la Guerra Street. Upstairs, a loggia overlooks the Plaza and the adobe-era pepper tree, which is a city landmark.

In 1922, the firm won the bid for the new high school. Their Spanish-Colonial design for the symmetrical, two-story

Santa Barbara County commissioned Sauter to design the Detention Center at 1015 Garden Street.

Sauter's design for Santa Barbara County National Bank (Courtesy of Rodney Sauter)

Postcard revealing the stripped-down embellishments of the new City Hall

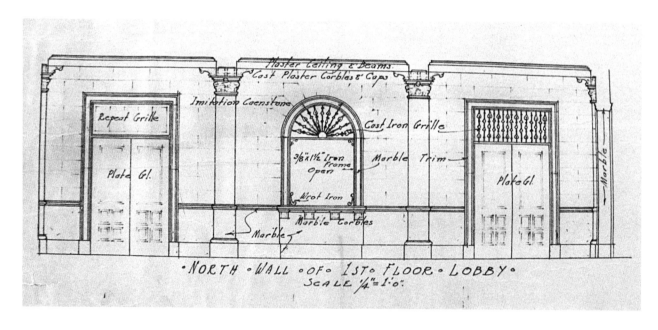

Details of ornamental designs for grillwork and columns of City Hall (UC Santa Barbara Architecture and Design Collection)

edifice incorporated churrigueresque surrounds on the main entrances. Arched windows, portals and arcades softened long sections of rectangular windows, and touches of iron grillwork accented the Spanish Revival style. The center of the building contained the auditorium, lobby, and entrance patio. The high school campus was completed in 1924, and the Class of '24 was the first to graduate from the new school, though they had attended no classes there.

Earthquake Remodels

By the mid 1920s, the humble farm boy from Maryland had made quite a mark on Santa Barbara architecture, designing scores of residences and several public buildings. In 1925 the firm was thriving, and as the morning of June 29 approached, Sauter and Lockard were about to become even busier.

The aftermath of the 6.8 magnitude earthquake that roared through Santa Barbara that morning left much of the city damaged if not completely devastated. The tower of

Sauter's First Presbyterian church crashed into the sanctuary, and its rebuilding removed much of the ornamental details. The quake created a huge market for architects and builders, however, and the Plans and Planting Committee was on hand to capitalize on the destruction of Victorian State Street and promote rebuilding in the Mediterranean and Spanish-Colonial style.

Sauter and Lockard were tried-and-true naturals for the job of redesigning and rebuilding the city in the preferred fashion. Sauter joined the city's Architectural Advisory committee to help other architects in the redesign of State Street, and the firm took on several projects as well.

In their remodel of the damaged three-story Fithian building, they removed its top story and all its ornamentation to transform it into a Spanish *edificio*. The Hotel Neal, built by hotelier Neal Callahan to match the 1905 Mission Revival train station on lower State Street, was remodeled into a more modern adaptation of Spanish architecture. The Tomlinson Building (710 State Street) no longer resembled a Victorian matron, thanks to Sauter & Lockhard, but looked sleek and new, clad in white stucco with a millinery of red tiles.

With the old Mascarel Hotel a complete loss due to the earthquake, Sauter and Lockard were free to design a new hotel in the Spanish Colonial style.

Undated rendering for Christian Church (Courtesy of Rodney Sauter)

PROPOSED CHRISTIAN CHVRCH
SANTA BARBARA CAL.

ROLAND F SAVTER 41517

Neal Callahan also owned the old Mascarel Hotel at State and Cota streets. The venerable Mascarel was a true victim of the earthquake and could not be revived with a few structural props and a facelift. Sauter & Lockard designed a U-shaped, four-story building of graceful arches and wrought-iron balconies enclosing a single story cloister-like lobby. Boasting 125 rooms, the hotel's amenities included a cigar stand, a barbershop, and a café. Fifty of the rooms came equipped with the latest technology—radio speakers connected to a central receiver.

As the years passed and the glory of the hotel faded, its name changed to the Schooner Inn, which garnered a reputation as an infamous flophouse. Today, the name is back to Hotel Barbara as millions of dollars' worth of restoration and renovation have returned it to quality status.

Cabrillo Pavilion

In 1925, David Gray had offered to build a beach pavilion for the city and hired Roland Sauter to design and build it. Delayed by the Santa Barbara earthquake, it was completed in 1927. When the city was unable to fulfill its promise to staff it, Gray offered to operate the pavilion at no profit to himself for the next five years. He convinced Roland Sauter to manage the enterprise, and Sauter operated his architectural business from his new office in town and from the Cabrillo Pavilion.

As a consequence of the earthquake, Sauter's plan included elements he believed would make the pavilion earthquake-proof. It was designed, of course, in the Spanish Colonial motif. Massive hand-hewn beams still support a red tile roof, Doric columns line the covered arcade, windows are arched or ornamented with recesses, and the balustrade on the second

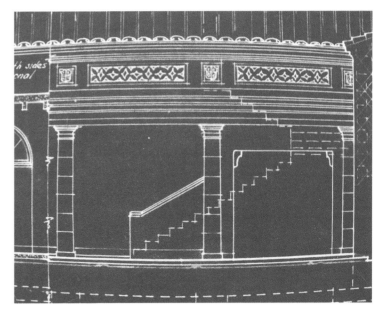

Architectural detail of design for the arcade of the Cabrillo Pavilion (UC Santa Barbara Architecture and Design Collection)

Sauter and his wife became managers of the Cabrillo Pavilion, shown here circa 1928.

Originally designated as the tea room, the main floor of the Cabrillo Pavilion continued to serve as a restaurant and dance hall for many years. The glass doors led to an outdoor balcony, and the interior balcony provided space for musicians or honored guests. (Courtesy of John Fritsche)

story promenade imitates Moorish screenwork. Extra touches included tiled flooring downstairs and lamps and other fixtures of wrought iron. All exposed metal fittings were of copper and all pipes of solid red brass.

The pavilion opened in May and by the July Independence Day festivities, its staff was challenged to manage its immense popularity. July 2 saw swimming races in front of the pavilion in the morning and a Santa Barbara Band concert in the afternoon. On Independence Day, enormous crowds descended on the pavilion balcony and beach to watch rockets, aerial bombs, fountains of fire, and pinwheels light up the night.

The *Morning Press* reported, "Cabrillo Pavilion was taxed to capacity all day and not a minute's rest did any of the employees get from Manager Roland F. Sauter down to the dishwasher." The pavilion sold out at 5,000 hot dogs, and the hectic pace of the day resulted in a pot of boiling water crashing to the floor and burning the feet of Sauter and another employee.

An August 1927 article says, "Every activity of the bath house is managed by Mr. Sauter." His wife Marty pitched in, too, and directed the enormously popular dances that were given every night of the week except Sundays. The pavilion, with its locker rooms and showers downstairs, became the center for water sports and beach activities.

Later years

By 1926, Sauter and Lockard had dissolved their partnership but each moved into new offices on East De la Guerra Street. Sauter occupied #107, which was conveniently located across from David Gray's office at the Meridian Studios across the street.

Sauter kept busy designing buildings such as those for City Meat Market at 1104 Chapala Street, Dal Pozzo Tire Corporation at 530 Chapala Street, and St. Paul Dye Works (now Ablitts) at 14 W. Gutierrez Street.

David Gray died in May 1928, and with his death and that of Clarence A. Black four years earlier, Sauter lost his two most important patrons. In 1928-29, he moved his office to the Granada Building. And though he presented a design for the Faulkner Art Gallery at the Santa Barbara Public Library, he again lost out to Myron Hunt and H.C. Chambers. Marty, meanwhile, fulfilled his role as acting manager of the Cabrillo Pavilion through 1931.

The Great Depression rocked the nation in 1929, and architectural commissions dried up. Sauter remodeled his home on Mission Ridge, dividing it into four apartments. In 1933, he designed a massive five-story apartment building complete with County Courthouse-style tower for the site behind his house. It was never built, but a cluster of two-story duplexes soon dotted the property, which became known as Mission Ridge Apartments. Marty became the manager, and Roland sought work elsewhere.

Sauter's design for the Faulkner Gallery addition skillfully incorporated and echoed elements of the existing architecture and provided a shaded arcade to complement the garden. (Courtesy of Rodney Sauter)

For a short time, Sauter's office was on the corner on *De la Guerra Street* and *Presidio Avenue*. Today, this simple building has been remodeled with additional *Spanish Revival* touches.

For the remainder of the economic crisis, Roland was employed by construction companies contracted with the Public Works Administration. He traveled as far as San Francisco and Los Angeles to find work. During World War II, he found employment as a contractor for the Eleventh Naval District in San Diego and as an architectural designer for the construction of the U.S. Army training center of Camp Cooke near Santa Maria. (Camp Cooke became Vandenberg Air Force Base in 1958.)

Roland Sauter died in 1951. Today, though few know his name, his vision and artistry have given Santa Barbara some of its most iconic landmarks. From stonework at the Mission to the buildings of City Hall, Barbara Hotel, and Santa Barbara High School to the Cabrillo Pavilion at the beach, we walk and drive by the evidence of his craft every day. Truly, he is an architect to be remembered.

Roland Sauter (Courtesy of Rodney Sauter)

Sauter's grand plan for his apartment complex never materialized. (Courtesy of Rodney Sauter)

Sources of Information

Buffalo Bill and His Wild West Show: Sources: contemporary local newspapers, various articles from the Buffalo Bill Historical Center website

Great White Fleet: Sources: Contemporary news articles, www.greatwhitefleet.info/, www.history.navy.mil/faqs/faq42-1.htm.

King Albert of Belgium's Sojourn: Sources: contemporary news articles in *Morning Press* and *New York Times*; articles by Stella Haverland Rouse and Walker Tompkins; *Noticias* 1963; the *Memoirs of Herbert Hoover*, Book 2, Chapter 2

McKinley Madness: Sources: contemporary news articles; *Santa Barbara – 1898-1925- as seen by a boy* by Edward Selden Spaulding; *My Santa Barbara Scrapbook* by Elizabeth Eaton Burton.

Teddy Roosevelt Rides to Town: Sources: contemporary news articles; Edward Selden Spaulding, *Santa Barbara as Seen by a Boy*; Henry F. Pringle, *Theodore Roosevelt*; Walker Tompkins, *The Yankee Barbarenos*; "The Hollister Family" by J.J. Hollister III, *Noticias* summer 1988

Cold Spring Canyon: Sources: contemporary news articles; maps, BLM homestead records; "Mountain Trails" by Jim Blakley in *Noticias,* Santa Barbara Historical Museum publication*;* the research of Barbara Goll and the late Jim Blakley and Maria Herold; *Montecito and Santa Barbara* by David Myrick; http://www.sblandtrust.org/portfolio-item/mar-cel-montecito/ -- accessed March 26, 2016)

Reaching for La Cumbre: Sources: Chamber of Commerce brochure of 1906; article by Gregory King in *Condor Call* of October 1982; various articles by Stella Haverland Rouse; "Santa Barbara As Seen by a Boy," by Edward Selden Spaulding; BLM land patent #3629; contemporary news articles; historical maps; the files of the late Jim Blakley, now part of the Santa Barbara Historical Museum archives.)

Montecito's Hot Springs Canyon: Sources not mentioned in text: Alfred Robinson's 1846 memoir, *Life in California;* articles by Stella Haverland Rouse; *Mineral Spring and Health Resorts of California,* 1892; vertical file on "Hot Springs" at the Santa Barbara Historical Museum; historic maps; "The Montecito Hot Springs Experience" by Klara Spinks Fleming, *Noticias*, Spring 1980; *News-Press,* 26 December 1989; Southwourth's *Santa Barbara and Montecito,* 1920; David Myrick's *Montecito and Santa Barbara;* city directories, U.S. Census

Up and Over Romero Canyon: Sources: *Mission Santa Barbara* by Maynard Geiger, O.F.M; *Historical Overview of Los Padres National Forest* by E.R. "Jim" Blakley and Karen Barnette; *Santa Barbara and Montecito* by David Myrick; oral history interviews with Albert Cottam and Eleanor Cottam; U.S. Census; city directories; Ancestry.com information; interview with Jim Andros, 2007; *News-Press* 17 January 1980.

Santa Barbara on Two Wheels: Sources: Contemporary news articles; http://caviews.com/EarlyCalPhoto.html; and various online histories of the bicycle

Auto Touring and Camping: Sources: contemporary news articles, Coleman Company website; camping articles from *Sunset Magazine* and its earlier version *Touring Topics.*

Auto Transformation: Sources: Contemporary news articles; city directories; Community Development files at UCSB Library, Special Collections; *Montecito and Santa Barbara* by David Myrick; Phillips *History of Santa Barbara County*; O'Neill's *History of Santa Barbara County*; U.S. Census; "Santa Barbara County Planning Commission" by Eric P. Hvolboll, *Noticias* Spring 1985; Minutes of the Santa Barbara County Planning Commission--various--1927-1938

Auto Mania: Sources: contemporary news articles; *Alice's Drive,* annotated by Gregory M. Franzwa; city directories; obituaries

The Unexpected Dr. Jane Edna Spaulding: Most of the information on Jane's time on Kelleys Island comes from **Leslie Korenko**, whose research into the history of the Island's pioneers has spawned several books and collected hundreds of early photographs. She was an invaluable mine of information and is much appreciated. Her website is http://www.kelleysislandstory.com. Other sources include U.S. and Kansas Census; contemporary articles in the local papers; Santa Barbara city directories; contemporary *New York Times* articles; Ancestry.com; Thompson and West p 171; http://www.homeoint.org/cazalet/histo/newyork.htm; Kansas State Historical Society website; Santa Fe Trails Research Library; Cottage Hospital annual reports. Special thanks also to **Debbie Gore** of the Jordaan Library in Larned, Kansas; to **Pam Hawes** of the Historical Association of Lewiston, New York; and to **Glenn Dubock**, CHS Media Services Coordinator, and **Ron Werft**, President and CEO of Cottage Health System.

The Parks of Park Lane: Sources: Ancestry.com records; obituaries; news clippings from Montecito Association History Archive; contemporary *Morning Press* articles; Little Town Club pamphlets; *Birth of the American Crucible Steel Industry* by Harrison Gilmer, 1953; http://www.sptddog.com/sotp/jomu.html, accessed 17 September 2016; *Montecito and Santa Barbara* by David Myrick; *El Pueblo Viejo* by Rebecca Conard and Christopher H. Nelson. With special thanks to Eleanor Park Beronius for passing along photographs and information of her great grandparents.

The Cultural Legacy of the Herter Family: Sources: The El Mirasol files of the late Muriel Osterhaus; contemporary news articles; Ancestry.com; *Herter Brothers: Furniture for a Gilded Age* by Katherine Howe, et al.; *Wellseley College: Report of the President 1930-31;* "El Mirasol: From Swan to Albatross" by Hattie Beresford in *Noticias,* spring 2001; *Art and Artists of Southern California*; *California Arts and Architecture*; "A Short History of Tapestry" by Eloise Samson Vaughan; contemporary newspaper articles; Name file at the Gledhill Library of the Santa Barbara Historical Museum; "A Tradition of Excellence: CAMA's History Book," CAMA, 2013/2014

Alexander Harmer, Painter of Spanish California: Main Sources: *Material Dreams* by Kevin Starr; contemporary news articles of events and exhibitions from Santa Barbara *Morning Press, New York Times, San Francisco Call*; city directories; "The Passing of the Nations" by S.E.A. Higgins, *Sunset* Magazine, Aug. 1903; U.S. Census information; California State Library card; "A Painter of Old California" by Charles F. Lummis, *Land of Sunshine*, December 1899; *California of the South,* Vol V, pp165-170, by John. S. McGroaty; 1982 exhibition catalog by James M. Hansen; Undated interview with Inez Harmer Northrup by Rosario Curletti; Sanborn Fire Insurance Maps; Sharpless Family Genealogy on Ancestry.com

Roland Sauter, Santa Barbara Architect: Sources: *El Pueblo Viejo* by Rebecca Conard and Christopher H. Nelson, 1986*; History of Santa Barbara, San Luis Obispo, and Ventura Counties* by Charles M. Gidney, 1917; contemporary news articles; Stella Haverland Rouse, *News-Press*, 27 April 1975; City Planning files; Obituaries; Ablitt's Website; Michael Redmon, *Santa Barbara Independent* 16 November 2011; Census and other Ancestry.com information; city directories; David Gebhard's *Santa Barbara: The Creation of a New Spain in America;* Architecture and Design Library at UCSB, Santa Barbara County Board of Supervisor's Minutes. **Many thanks to Rodney Sauter**, Roland F. Sauter's grandnephew, for sharing the information, photos, and artifacts in his possession.

Index